I0103006

On Your Mark, Get Set...
Tourism's Take-Off in Micronesia

FRANCIS X. HEZEL, SJ

EAST-WEST CENTER

EAST-WEST CENTER

The East-West Center promotes better relations and understanding among the people and nations of the United States, Asia, and the Pacific through cooperative study, research, and dialogue. Established by the US Congress in 1960, the Center serves as a resource for information and analysis on critical issues of common concern, bringing people together to exchange views, build expertise, and develop policy options.

The Center's 21-acre Honolulu campus, adjacent to the University of Hawai'i at Mānoa, is located midway between Asia and the US mainland and features research, residential, and international conference facilities. The Center's Washington, DC, office focuses on preparing the United States for an era of growing Asia Pacific prominence.

EastWestCenter.org

Print copies are available from Amazon.com. Single copies of most titles can be downloaded from the East-West Center website, at EastWestCenter.org.

For information, please contact:

Publications Office
East-West Center
1601 East-West Road
Honolulu, Hawai'i 96848-1601

Telephone: 808.944.7197

EWCBooks@EastWestCenter.org
EastWestCenter.org/Publications

ISBN 978-0-86638-280-9 (print) and 978-0-86638-281-6 (electronic)

© 2017 East-West Center

On Your Mark, Get Set...Tourism's Take-Off in Micronesia
Francis X. Hezel, SJ

A tourist photographs Chuukese children playing at the shore near a World War II–era wreck. *Photograph by Tim Rock.*

Table of Contents

Executive Summary

When Continental Air Micronesia inaugurated regular jet air service to the Trust Territory of the Pacific Islands in the late 1960s, it created new links between the Islands and both the US mainland and East Asia. The new flight service opened commercial possibilities for islands then struggling with an uncertain political and economic future. Tourism was at best a distant hope as an engine for economic growth. Chuuk, Marshall Islands, Northern Marianas, Palau, Pohnpei, and Yap all began promoting tourism at the same time, with roughly comparable infrastructure and a total of 238 hotel rooms among them. In 1970, Continental built three new 50-room hotels in Chuuk, Palau, and the Northern Marianas and began vigorously promoting the islands as a Pacific paradise getaway destination. What happened over subsequent decades in these three island groups is the subject of this study.

The Northern Marianas, mainly the principal island of Saipan, began to develop a rapidly expanding Japanese visitor market in the early 1970s. The proximity to Japan and slightly superior infrastructure may have aided its comparatively early development of tourism. By 1996, Saipan was welcoming nearly three-quarters of a million tourists yearly. The 1997 Asian economic crisis, along with land-lease issues and the alienation of a major Asian carrier, subsequently contributed to a dramatic downturn in tourism. After partially rebounding in 2003 on the strength of a vibrant Korean market, an airline crash a decade later resulted in a second major downturn. The Commonwealth of the Northern Mariana Islands (CNMI) has still not fully recovered from these shocks, although visitor numbers have shown encouraging growth in recent years.

In Palau, the tourism industry had a much slower start than in the Northern Marianas. It was only with the completion of its first luxury hotel in 1985, built in partnership with a Japanese investor, that tourism first took off. The market, originally heavily Japanese, diversified in time to include Koreans, Taiwanese, and more recently mainland Chinese. Dramatic increases in tourists from China during the past several years have expanded the total to over 150,000 visitors yearly. But the tourist boom has increasingly strained facilities and threatened unique environmental attractions. Today Palau is the only Pacific nation implementing policies to reduce total visitor arrivals while attracting more high-value clientele.

Institutional dynamics and infrastructure may not be the most important prerequisites for the complex process of tourism development

Chuuk experienced an initial limited surge in tourism because of its appeal to divers interested in exploring the sunken Japanese "ghost ships" from World War II. This proved to be a narrow niche market, however, and tourist numbers over the next 40 years never grew beyond a few thousand a year. Although visitor numbers are slightly higher in Chuuk than in other states of the Federated States of Micronesia, the country has yet to realize the economic benefits it once hoped for from tourism. Its distance from principal Asian markets and higher airfare may be the main factors in its failure to expand the industry.

Taken together, the three case studies suggest that institutional dynamics and infrastructure may not be the most important prerequisites for the complex process of tourism development. Convenient location, strong commercial linkages with a solid start-up market (e.g., Japan), and reliable air service seem to be among the most important factors at work in the success of Palau and the Northern Marianas. As tourism markets mature, other factors become critical —especially the availability of land for development and the readiness of the island nation to respond rapidly to new opportunities. Even so, there remains an element of serendipity to tourism growth that should not be dismissed.

Policymakers elsewhere in the Pacific may reasonably look to tourism as a catalyst for national economic development, but what these case studies suggest is that they should not assume all Pacific states can successfully summon a tourist industry at will. Moreover, since tourism is a highly mobile and competitive economic activity, the gains made in nurturing an emerging tourism industry can fluctuate almost overnight due to global forces well beyond the control of island governments or investors.

The Pacific Island Nations

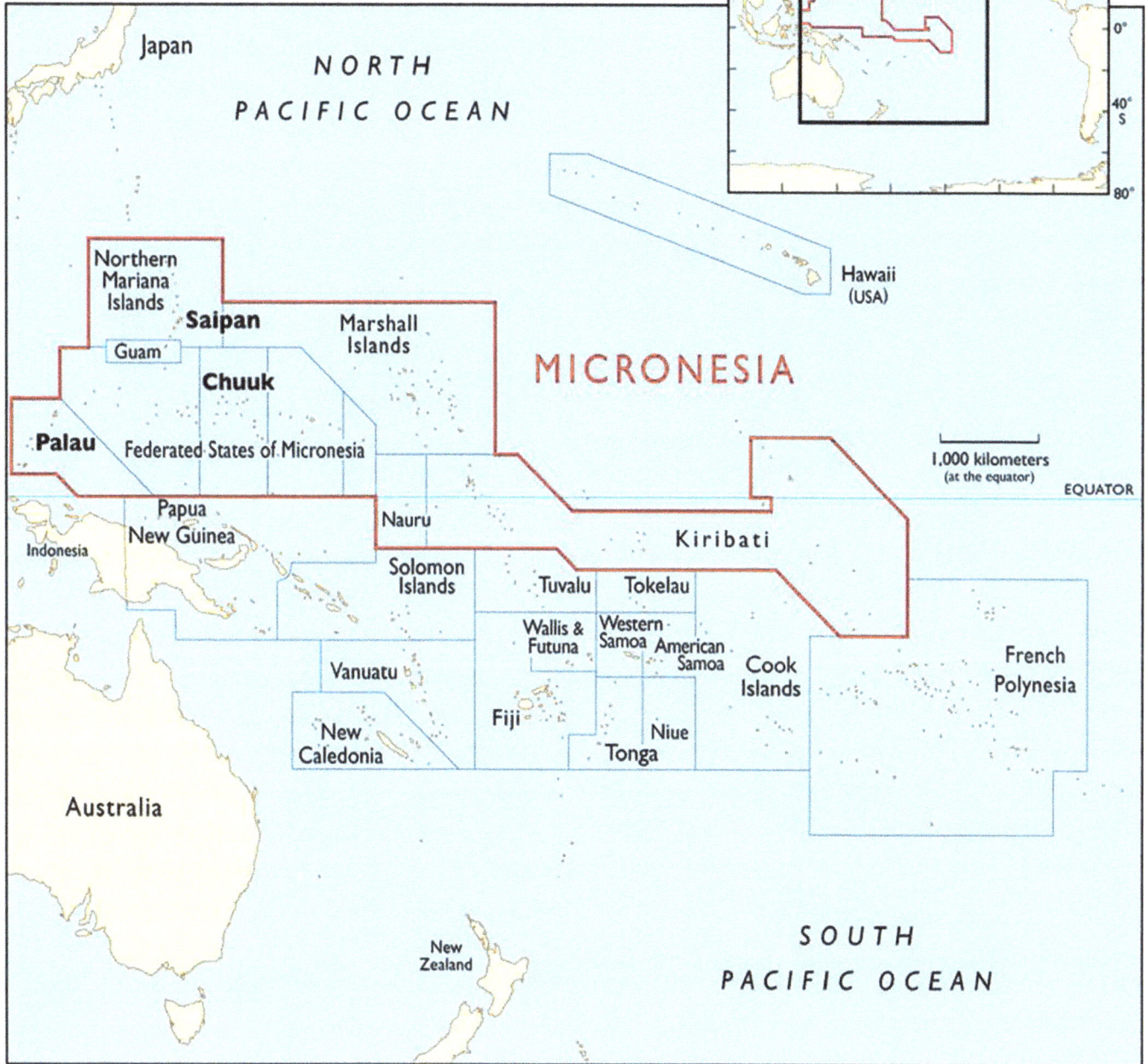

Japan

NORTH

PACIFIC OCEAN

Hawaii
(USA)

Northern
Mariana
Islands

Saipan

Guam

Marshall
Islands

MICRONESIA

Chuuk

Palau

Federated States of Micronesia

1,000 kilometers
(at the equator)

EQUATOR

Indonesia

Papua
New Guinea

Nauru

Kiribati

Solomon
Islands

Tuvalu

Tokelau

Wallis &
Futuna

Western
Samoa

American
Samoa

Vanuatu

French
Polynesia

Cook
Islands

Fiji

New
Caledonia

Niue

Tonga

Australia

New
Zealand

SOUTH

PACIFIC OCEAN

120°E

0°

120°W

60° 80°

40°
N

0°

40°
S

80°

A map of Continental Air Micronesia routes published sometime between 1968 and 1974. From the Pacific Collection, Hamilton Library, University of Hawaiʻi at Mānoa.

On Your Mark, Get Set...
Tourism's Take-Off in Micronesia

Introduction

TOURISM: HOPE FOR THE HAVE-NOTS

The Pacific Islands labor under exceptional difficulties in attempting to grow self-sustaining economies in the global community today. They are small, distant from major world markets, and lack the resources that could be profitably traded for the foreign exchange so necessary for life today. Their size and remoteness generally rule out commercial agriculture, while other factors preclude manufacturing. Unless Pacific Island nations happen to be blessed with rich mineral deposits, as was once the case with Nauru (phosphate) and is so even today with Papua New Guinea (gold, copper, and natural gas), they find that none of the traditional avenues of economic growth are open to them.

Tourism may be viewed, then, as the last resort of these economically challenged and resource-poor Pacific nations. If all else fails, perhaps tourism will come to their rescue. After all, tourism has a way of turning liabilities into assets. An island group may be small, remote, and without resources—perhaps it might even be described as backward—but all of that simply adds to its allure and distinguishes it as an exotic getaway. Such islands have a history of becoming prime tourist destinations—for instance, many of the Caribbean islands, the Seychelles, and Guam. Hawai'i, which has seen its sugar and pineapple production fall off over the years, has been a major getaway destination for half a century or longer.[1] So, tourism has become the hope of those islands without anything else to drive their economy.

Is the hope of a tourism-based economy realistic for Pacific Island nations or is it an illusion? What is needed, besides sun, sand, and sea, to develop tourism? The prescription for tourism has already been written, but the formula is much like that for generating any kind of successful economy.[2] Even if these changes have been made—that is, long-term land leases, favorable conditions for foreign investors, an equitable justice system—will a strong tourist industry necessarily follow?

Instead of simply accepting these a priori, we decided to do a historical study of a few places in the Pacific that might have been candidates for a booming tourist industry. We looked at three spots in the northwestern Pacific—two independent nations along with an island group that has become a commonwealth under the United States—to see what contributed to the rise of a successful tourist industry or perhaps inhibited it, how obstacles were dealt with, and what factors might have weighed most heavily in the outcome. In following a historical approach, we were simply trying to capture how different islands responded to the concrete challenges that growing a tourist industry presented.

The three island groups used as case studies here—Palau, Chuuk, and the Northern Mariana Islands—share a number of common characteristics. All these island groups are located in the western Pacific north of the equator in that sector of the region known as Micronesia. The islands share key physical characteristics as well: Each is an island group rather than a single land mass, each group has a very limited land area, and each is blessed with all the tropical features that are commonly sought by those seeking a vacation in the Pacific. All three also have a shared history of colonial rule.

HISTORY OF THE THREE ISLAND GROUPS

Before the late nineteenth century, Spain was the only nation with colonial interests in the western Pacific north of the equator. At the height of its power 300 years earlier, Spain had begun using the Mariana Islands as a way station to the Philippines in the trans-Pacific galleon trade. Finally, Spain had taken possession of the island group in the late 1600s and established a colonial government there. Soon afterward, the people of Saipan and its neighboring islands in the northern part of the chain were resettled on Guam, and for the following century and a half these islands were largely uninhabited (Hezel 1989).

Only in the late nineteenth century did Spain make any attempt to take possession of other islands in that part of the Pacific. In 1886 Spain annexed the Caroline Islands, an archipelago that includes both Palau at the extreme west and Chuuk much farther east. With this annexation a century of colonial rule commenced for the Caroline Islands.[3] At just about the same time, Saipan was slowly being repopulated as Carolinian seafarers and Chamorros from Guam drifted north to take up residence in Saipan and nearby islands (Russell 1984).

After its defeat in the Spanish-American War, Spain was forced to sell its island possessions to Germany in 1899. From that time on, Palau, Chuuk, and the Northern Mariana Islands (of which Saipan was the capital) would be united under a succession of foreign powers: Germany, Japan, and the United States.[4] The three island groups would remain politically bound together until the inception of their self-government in the 1970s.

At the outbreak of the World War I, Japan swooped into Germany's island possessions in Micronesia to claim them for itself. Its claim was legitimized at the end of the war when Japan was entrusted with the administration of the islands of Micronesia as a League of Nations mandate. Over the course of its 30-year tenure, Japan left a lasting legacy in the islands. Even today the local languages contain hundreds of Japanese loan words for everything from carpentry tools to baseball terms. Likewise, Japan made a permanent imprint on the cuisine of island people, to say nothing of other features of life. The size of the Japanese population was considerable in each of the three island groups: 20,000 in the Northern Marianas, 10,000 in Palau, and 3,500 in Chuuk (Hezel 1995, 190). Chuuk was the only group of the three in which the local population was not heavily outnumbered by Japanese nationals before the war. After war broke out, the number of Japanese expanded greatly as additional troops were assigned to defend the islands.

World War II's impact on the islands was enormous everywhere, but in different ways from one island group to the next. Allied Forces bombarded and invaded Palau and Saipan in 1944, a year before the end of the war. Suicide Cliff and Banzai Cliff on Saipan, sites of mass suicides by Japanese civilians as American troops advanced north, were later memorialized as shrines. The beaches and caves on the islands of Angaur and Peleliu in Palau, where fierce fighting took

World War II's impact on the islands was enormous everywhere, but in different ways from one island group to the next

place, are now reverenced as historical monuments. Chuuk, on the other hand, was subjected to several intense bombing raids but was never invaded.

Even when Japanese survivors were repatriated at the end of the war, this did not signal the end of the influence of Japan on the islands they once occupied. There remained at least the memories, if not the ruins, of the geisha houses, bars, movie theaters, and baseball fields from the height of the Japanese era.

The end of the war brought a new colonial authority over the islands—the United States, administering the islands as a trust territory for the newly founded United Nations. US rule ushered in an era of peace but not prosperity, since the governing principle during those years was to avoid disrupting the traditional island lifestyle by introducing rapid modernization. Marginal jobs, largely in the government sector, were available for a few local people, but most islanders supported themselves from the land and the sea as they always had. The largest export at the time was copra, just as it had been 80 years earlier (Hezel 1995, 282–296).

It was only in the early 1960s during the presidency of John F. Kennedy that the first serious attempts were made to modernize the Trust Territory. The United States expanded the yearly subsidies to the islands for development of education and health facilities and for infrastructure, most notably roads and airports. The number of jobs multiplied during those years, many of them going to Micronesians, and so did local interest in self-government. Political self-rule, only then emerging in other parts of the Pacific, became a topic of keen public discussion for the first time (Hezel 1995, 297–311). As Micronesia began scanning its political horizon and exploring future options, the question of what could be done to develop the island economy in the future also came to the fore.

At about the same time, the once-cloistered Trust Territory was opened up to the world. During the 1950s special permission had been required to visit the territory, and about the only ones who stopped off there were government officials and missionaries. Air service was once a week, usually by an amphibious SA-16 that carried only 15 passengers and whatever mail would fit in the cargo hold. The emergence of Micronesia onto the world stage was best symbolized by the inauguration of Air Micronesia, offering as it did the first dependable air service to the islands.

In 1968 Continental Airlines began service in the western Pacific, taking over the old Pan Am routes even as it expanded flights in the area. Air Micronesia (or Air Mike, as the Continental subsidiary was called) provided the air service to bring in visitors from as far away as Asia and the continental United States. One local historian claimed without exaggeration that the airline's foundation "was probably the single most important factor in the future development of what were once remote and isolated islands in the Pacific" (Stewart 2005). As the former Trust Territory head of tourism succinctly put it, "With the establishment of Air Micronesia tourism was born" (Ashman 1974, 135). The same year saw other major innovations by the Trust Territory government that would assist. "New commercial air and sea contracts were signed. Entry requirements were liberalized and travel agents began to take interest in the world's newest "destination area" (TT 1969).

With a regional airline in operation and a rapid development program underway in the territory, the stage was set for the initiation of a tourist industry. Moreover, all the districts of the Trust Territory were at roughly the same level of advancement in the late 1960s. Hence, Palau, Chuuk, and the Northern Marianas—the three island groups used here for our case studies—would have left the starting gate at about the same time in their search for tourism.

In the 1960s the question of what could be done to develop the island economy in the future came to the fore

SEPARATE POLITICAL PATHS

In the meantime, various forces began driving the islands, once united under a common government imposed on them by a succession of colonial powers, in separate directions. Cultural and linguistic differences were reasserting themselves as the six districts seriously began to weigh their post-colonial prospects for the first time. Added to this were differences in the value of these different island groups to the United States.

By the early 1970s, just a few years after its first legislative body was formed, the Trust Territory (sometimes known simply as Micronesia) was beginning to splinter. For years, the Northern Marianas had viewed itself as the most developed part of the Trust Territory, much more closely linked to Guam by virtue of its culture and language than to the other island groups in the territory. The Northern Marianas also knew that the United States took special interest in the strategic value that these islands represented. Contributing to this strategic interest were the proximity of the Northern Marianas to Guam, the suitability of the flat island of Tinian for military training exercises, and the desire of the United States to have a backup airfield for Guam. In 1975, the Northern Mariana Islands, with Saipan as its capital, initiated a close relationship with the United States under a new covenant that would formally make them a commonwealth.[5]

The next few years saw a rapid breakup of the remainder of the Trust Territory as the other districts hurried toward a resolution of their own political status. After all, Micronesia had always been a mélange of different cultural units held together by colonial rule. By the late 1970s, Palau, at the extreme western end of the Trust Territory, broke ranks with its neighbors to become a separate nation, while the Marshalls, at the eastern end, did the same.

Palau and the Marshalls were undoubtedly prompted to split off because of the critical advantages these two island groups held in dealing with the United States.[6] Leaders in these two groups hoped to rely on these advantages to spur their economic growth in the future. In the case of Palau, the United States had expressed interest in staging military training exercises on the large island of Babeldaob, and possibly in utilizing other parts of the island group as well. Palau was well positioned to play a key role in the fallback strategy for the United States as it sought to reposition the military bases that had once been lodged around the perimeter of East Asia.

This left the remaining island groups (Chuuk, Pohnpei, Kosrae, and Yap) to form the Federated States of Micronesia. By 1979, just four years after the Northern Marianas was recognized as a US commonwealth, self-government was put in place for the Federated States of Micronesia (FSM), Palau, and the Marshall Islands. Constitutions were adopted for these political units, presidents were elected, and legislative bodies were vested with decision-making power. Because of delays in Washington, the Compact of Free Association was only formally inaugurated some years later—in 1986 for the FSM and the Marshalls Islands, and in 1994 for Palau.[7]

In the end, the FSM and Palau, along with the Marshall Islands, were recognized as fully independent nations and were offered membership in the United Nations. Yet, they were also bound to the United States by a treaty known as the Compact of Free Association. Under the terms of this agreement, the United States offered these new nations the funding they needed during their initial economic-development phase, in theory until the nations become fully self-reliant. In return for this, the FSM and the other Compact nations provide the United States with unrestricted access to airspace and shipping lanes as well as to the islands themselves.

By the early 1970s, the Trust Territory was beginning to splinter

Consequently, because of Compact dollars from the United States, the FSM and Palau have achieved full self-government even without the self-sufficient economy that normally under-writes the full expenses of government.

WHAT FOLLOWS

Pacific nations (or even non-independent appendages of a major power) are constantly on the search for anything that will drive their economies. The sale of territorial rights, whether in the form of lease of fishing rights to foreign nations or provision of military bases, is one answer. Another is tourism, which involves provision of short-term access for foreigners who want to enjoy beaches, weather, and cultural ambience. Micronesian islands are as much in need of an economic engine as any other part of the Pacific.[8]

In the body of this study we will present the story of three Micronesian island groups, each originally rated as a strong prospect for tourism, and show how the search for a tourism industry has unfolded in each. In the course of this story we hope to present more than simply the outcome; we hope to capture the exchanges between the island groups and outside forces, revealing the dynamics at work between them and how they affected later developments.

The final chapter will assess the major factors involved in the growth of tourism in the three island groups selected and offer suggestions regarding which factors have played the most critical roles in fostering this industry.

REFERENCES

Ashman, Mike. 1974. "Micronesia Tastes Tourism," in *A New Kind of Sugar: Tourism in the Pacific*, eds. Ben Finney and Karen Ann Watson, 135–143. Honolulu: The East-West Center.

Duncan, Ron, Sandy Cuthbertson, and Malcolm Bosworth. 1999. *Pursuing Economic Reform in the Pacific*. Pacific Studies Series, no. 18. Manila: Asian Development Bank.

Hezel, Francis X. 1989. *From Conquest to Colonization: Spain in the Mariana Islands 1690–1740*. Occasional Historical Papers Series, no. 2. Saipan: Northern Marianas Division of Historic Preservation.

———. 1995. *Strangers in Their Own Land: A Century of Colonial Rule in the Caroline and Marshall Islands*. Pacific Islands Monograph Series, no. 13. Honolulu: University of Hawai'i Press.

———. 2012. *Pacific Island Nations: How Viable Are Their Economies?* Pacific Islands Policy, no. 7. Honolulu: East-West Center. www.eastwestcenter.org/publications/pacific-island-nations-how-viable-are-their-economies.

Mak, James. 2008. *Developing a Dream Destination: Tourism and Tourism Policy Planning in Hawai'i*. Honolulu: University of Hawai'i Press.

McHenry, Donald. 1975. *Micronesia: Trust Betrayed*. New York: Carnegie Endowment for International Peace.

Russell, Scott. 1984. *From Arabwal to Ashes: A Brief History of Garapan Village—1818 to 1945.* Micronesian Archaeological Survey Report, no. 19. Saipan: Northern Marianas Division of Historic Preservation.

Trust Territory Government. 1969. "Tourism Status Report for the Year January–December 1969." Saipan: Department of Resources and Development.

TT. *See* Trust Territory Government.

NOTES

[1] On Hawai'i's historical development as a major tourist destination, see Mak 2008.

[2] One of the classic formulations of the requirements for economic development in the Pacific can be found in Duncan et al. 1999.

[3] For a history of the Spanish takeover and the ensuing history of colonial rule in the region, see Hezel 1995.

[4] Guam, the southernmost island in the Marianas archipelago, was retained by the United States after Spain's defeat in the Spanish-American War. Thereafter, the Northern Marianas and Guam, although bound together by a common language and culture, followed different political trajectories.

[5] The separation of the Northern Mariana Islands is treated briefly in Hezel 1995: 335–337, but much more fully in McHenry 1975: 130–169.

[6] The strategic value of both island groups had long been recognized by the Japanese, and by American troops retaking Japanese-held islands in the final year of the World War II. Rather than bypassing the Marshalls and Palau, as they did the rest of the Carolines, US troops invaded both places because of the assets they offered.

[7] The delay in the formal approval of Palau's Compact was due to US insistence that the Palau Constitution be amended to remove the article forbidding the passage of nuclear or chemical weapons through Palau waters. This took several years and seven referenda to accomplish.

[8] A look at the economies of Micronesian island groups compared with other Pacific nations is offered in Hezel 2012.

Chuuk Tourism

CHUUK TODAY

"Diver's Haven" is the inscription on license plates in Chuuk, the most populous of the four states in the Federated States of Micronesia (FSM). Billed as the world's greatest wreck-diving destination, Chuuk's 40-mile-wide lagoon is the resting place of more than 50 Japanese ships sunk during Allied bombing raids in World War II. These hulks, which have been transformed into ship reefs over the years, offer a brilliant display of multicolored hard and soft corals that have been fused onto the hulls and decks of the fleet. The wrecks, with their combination of picturesque undersea life and military artifacts, provide spectacular diving sites for enthusiasts.

Aside from its magnificent wreck diving, however, Chuuk has little by way of unique assets to attract visitors to this distant island group. Chuuk, a cluster of elevated islands enclosed in a large lagoon and surrounded by other islands that are part of the state, has all the natural beauty and charm popularly associated with the Pacific. But so do many other destinations that are easier and cheaper to reach. The local people are charming and warm and everything that Pacific Islanders are expected to be. But the same can be said of people throughout the whole area.

Chuuk has features that could be turned into tourist attractions. At the southern end of the main island, on the grounds of the largest hotel, a museum on World War II in the Pacific has been built. At another end of the island, a Japanese-built lighthouse offering a commanding view of the lagoon is open to visitors. Chuuk Visitors Bureau cited spots on other islands that

A diver explores the rich coral cover on the WWII shipwreck *Shinkoko Maru* in Chuuk Lagoon, Federated States of Micronesia. *Photograph by Tim Rock.*

could be developed, such as the Japanese historic sites on the island of Tonoas—the old town that flourished during the 1920s and 1930s, the naval base that served the wartime Japanese fleet, and the old Japanese-built hospital later used as a jail. Everywhere, there are beautiful beaches, steep hills to climb, and even a few interesting waterfalls.

Weno, the small triangular-shaped main island in Chuuk Lagoon, has an area of seven square miles and a population of about 14,000—about a third of the population of the state. It is the state capital, the business center of Chuuk, and the site of the airport, where, each month, the single airline serves some 500 visitors who arrive and 200 local residents who leave for good.

The islands may be blessed with natural beauty—a bright display of earth and plant colors that are merely a warm-up for the dazzling sights to be seen underwater. Even so, no one would call Weno a welcoming spot for tourists. Visitors are immediately confronted with abundant evidence of decay: abandoned buildings covered with graffiti, cement shells of old stores and other once-prosperous businesses, and shuttered homes with boarded windows. In place of stone fences or even the traditional rough-cut wooden poles, rusted and wrinkled sheets of tin roofing surround homes, both abandoned and inhabited. The roads, once paved but never maintained, are rutted and pitted with what look like shell craters. Traffic crawls along, often at a pace slower than a leisurely walk, with drivers weaving their way from one side of the road to another to avoid the deepest potholes. The old joke told here is that in other places police may identify the drunken driver as the guy who swerves this way and that, but in Chuuk he has to be the guy who doesn't.

The island has its magic spots. Xavier High School, perched in the saddle of a chain of hills that was formerly the site of a Japanese naval communications center. The churches, Catholic and Protestant, are attractive and well maintained. There is the Japanese gun emplacement half-way up one of the mountains, and the knobby peak of Tonaachaw, the neighboring mountain, once believed to be enchanted. But, overall, much of the island of Weno has the appearance of a shantytown.

The single airline serves some 500 visitors who arrive each month and 200 residents who leave for good

CHUUK: A STATE IN THE FEDERATED STATES OF MICRONESIA

Chuuk is one of the four states of the FSM, an island nation comprising the chain of islands running east–west just above the equator in the western Pacific. Formerly the geographical center of the Trust Territory of the Pacific that was administered by the United States from the end of World War II, the FSM became self-governing in 1980 and fully independent in 1986. Today the FSM consists of four separate states—Chuuk, Pohnpei, Kosrae, and Yap—each with its own governor and legislature and an unusually high degree of political autonomy.

The FSM constitution was originally written as a compromise document that would offer those states considering nationhood on their own an attractive option of semi-autonomy within the federation. But even such a constitution, with its loose binding to the central government, failed to keep Palau and the Marshalls from seceding and following their own political fortunes.[1] It has, however, provided a political framework for the remaining states that can legitimately be described as a federation. The states are represented in the national government and receive their allotment of Compact funds from it, but they manage their own affairs for the most part without much oversight by the federal government.

Chuuk, with its population of 50,000, has as many people as the other three states combined. Located near the center of the string of islands that make up the FSM, Chuuk was at one time considered as the possible capital for the new nation, but its dense population and the legendary difficulty of finding available land ruled it out. Instead, Pohnpei was made the capital.

BEGINNINGS OF TOURISM

In the late 1960s, a decade before the effective end of the Trust Territory administration, the United States had greatly expanded its budget to help the islands modernize, schools and hospitals were improved, and talk of political self-government was very much in the air. Thanks to the expansion of government services, job opportunities for local people were multiplying. All that seemed missing on this trajectory toward the future were the underpinnings of a viable economy. Exports were understandably few, given the scant resources to be found in the islands. Copra exports of $2 million a year represented the biggest source of productive income for the Trust Territory (Hezel 1984, 53).

Then in 1968, Continental Air Micronesia began service in the region and opened new routes through the islands. For the first time, flights connected the islands directly to Guam and Hawai'i, not just once a week, as had been the case when Pan Am operated the service, but two or three times weekly. With the new airline in place, the Trust Territory government declared that it was making a major commitment to the development of tourism. As one of the first Trust Territory tourism reports explained, "New commercial air and sea transport contracts were signed. Entry requirements were liberalized and travel agents began to take interest in the world's newest 'destination area'" (TT 1969, 1). Tourism seemed to hold great promise for islands without any real economic engine.

The results during the first year of the new airline service looked encouraging. The number of visitors to the Trust Territory rose from 13,000 to 20,600 between 1968 and 1969, while 32,000 were projected for 1970 (TT 1969, 1). The new tourist industry generated just under $1 million by 1969 and had become the second largest source of revenue. A report on tourism at the end of 1969 proudly declared: "Micronesia—US Trust Territory of the Pacific Islands—is on the move. Its tourism industry now represents the Territory's major growth potential." The report envisioned 274,000 tourists by 1975 and an estimated income of $13 million if present trends continued (TT 1969, 1).

It is important to note that all six of the districts, as they were then called—the Northern Marianas, Palau, Yap, Chuuk, Pohnpei, and the Marshalls—left the gate at the same time in the race for tourism. Tourist facilities in the various districts were roughly comparable at that time. Pohnpei had three small hotels with a total of only about 20 rooms, Chuuk had two with 23 rooms, Yap had a single hotel (Rai View) with 10 rooms, the Marshalls had two hotels with 21 rooms, and Palau was served by three hotels with 35 rooms (TT 1970, 6–8). Even Saipan, the main island in the Marianas, had just two hotels with a total of 30 rooms before its first major hotel, the Royal Taga, with 60 first-class rooms and its state-of-the-art facilities, was opened in late 1969.[2] Poised as it was for the development of a growing tourist industry, the entire Trust Territory in 1969 had a total of 238 rooms for visitors, counting those places that hardly would deserve to have been called hotels (TT 1969, 1).

Tourism seemed to hold great promise for islands without any real economic engine

Visitor numbers in the Trust Territory rose sharply during the early 1970s, even if the numbers fell far short of the Trust Territory Tourism Bureau's optimistic predictions for 1975. Visitors for 1972 totaled 36,199; over the next three years they rose steadily from 47,115 in 1973, to 60,835 in 1974, and finally to 66,017 in 1975 (Table 1). During these years, Saipan, the principal island in the Marianas and the capital of the Trust Territory since the early 1960s, established itself as the "must-see" spot in the region. Even if the Royal Taga had never been built, other hotels would have taken advantage of the opportunity of the surge in tourism there. Of the 20,600 visitors to the Trust Territory in 1969, over 16,000 targeted the Marianas (TT 1969, 2). Between 1969 and 1975, the overwhelming majority of all visitors—between 60 and 70 percent—came to the Marianas.[3] In 1975, with its tourism growing rapidly, the Northern Marianas separated from the rest of the Trust Territory to become a commonwealth under the United States.

During the early 1970s, tourism was distributed rather equitably throughout the rest of the Trust Territory. Chuuk, Pohnpei, and Palau registered just over 4,000 visitors in 1973, with the Marshalls and Yap somewhat lower (US Dept. of State 1973). This was the case for the remainder of the decade and into the mid-1980s before Palau's tourism industry finally took its first substantial leap forward. Differences between the other island groups, which by that time had become the Federated States of Micronesia, remained very small.

Continental Airlines, which began operations in 1968, had already contributed to this initial burst of tourism when it expanded its routes and increased the number of flights. Two years later, it built new 50-room hotels on Saipan, Palau, and Chuuk.[4] Meanwhile, a new airstrip opened on Pohnpei in February 1970, allowing commercial airplanes to land at the island for the first time.

Many of those early visitors were from American soil: 66 percent of the visitors in 1969 came from the mainland United States, Hawai'i, and Guam. The Japanese market was just opening at the time, but it was already supplying 5,000 visitors, or 25 percent of the total (TT 1969, 1). The new affluence in Japan was propelling the tourism that would expand rapidly over the course of the next couple of decades.

EARLY SURGE IN CHUUK

When Continental Airlines announced its plans to put up a 50-room hotel near the popular beach at the southern tip of Weno, there was every reason to believe that this would be the impetus needed to get a good tourist industry underway. Chuuk was the closest island to Guam and had a decent landing field already in service. The island was well known for the role it played as a Japanese-fleet anchorage during the war; consequently, Chuuk had a cachet of sorts that most other island groups were without.

The early hospitality business was as basic in Chuuk as it was elsewhere in the territory. During the early Trust Territory years, from the 1950s through the mid-1960s, the place to stay for government travelers was the Truk Hotel, little more than a Quonset hut located next to the old Community Club in Nantaku, site of the present hospital. Later, during the 1960s, other hotels were opened. The Bayview, with its four rooms and family atmosphere, was frequented mainly by visitors doing business with the Mori family who owned it. Christy's Hotel, built by Christy Killion of Losap, offered 18 rooms in its downtown location but catered more to local people rather than foreign guests.

Many of those early visitors were from American soil; the Japanese market was just opening at the time

Perhaps the first place that could be genuinely called a commercial hotel was Hotel Maramar, started in 1969 and managed by an American couple, Russ and Verna Curtis. The Maramar had 19 rooms, 15 standard and 4 deluxe, and offered full dining services to its guests and local visitors. The facility provided unusual amenities, including excursions on a trimaran owned by the hotel and operated by a former Peace Corps volunteer (Clark Graham interview). The hotel survived only a few years, however, due to recurring land problems with the owners and the reputation for violence that the place soon acquired. A young Chuukese was stabbed there during a drinking session, and on another occasion gunshots were fired into a room by an angry or drunk passerby. The Maramar was closed in 1975 (Bill Stinnett interview).

Construction work on the new Continental Hotel began in 1969, and the 50-room hotel was opened the following year. Like the other hotels built by Continental Airlines, this was managed by TraveLodge. With the opening of the new Continental, the room capacity in Chuuk effectively tripled.

The number of visitors to Chuuk showed a steady upswing, thanks in part to improved flight schedules and the comfortable lodging that the new hotel afforded, not to mention the attention that Micronesia had received as a tourist destination because of the efforts of Continental Airlines. Between 1972 and 1978, yearly visitors nearly doubled, rising from 2,999 to 5,749 (Table 1). Chuuk's growth was paralleled by the other districts, especially Palau and Pohnpei. But by 1978, just as the Trust Territory was on the verge of finally becoming fully self-governing, tourism in what was to become the Federated States of Micronesia hit a plateau. Chuuk's tourism figures for 1978 (5,749 visitors) and 2013 (5,800 visitors) were virtually unchanged (Table 1). Notwithstanding its promising beginning, the tourist industry has stagnated in Chuuk, just as it has in the rest of the FSM, for 35 years.

ATTRACTION OF WRECK DIVING

The start of commercial wreck diving in Chuuk may have been directly linked with the opening of the new Continental Hotel. Soon after the hotel opened in 1970, some of the pilots on Air Micronesia flights began checking into the hotel so that they could spend a few days scuba diving between flights. For some of the pilots it became a routine that they would leave their scuba tanks and gear at the hotel in between stopovers. In those days, as one informant recalled, the tanks had to be refilled at the Office of Fisheries, which had the only compressor on the island (Bill Stinnett interview). It appears, then, that not only did Continental trigger wreck diving with its improved air service and its quality accommodations in Chuuk, but that the airline provided the first customers for the business.

Not only did Continental airlines trigger wreck diving with its air service and accommodations, but it also provided the first customers for the businesses

The Japanese sunken ships—or the "Ghost Fleet," as they have been termed—are recognized today as Chuuk's main claim to international fame. But it was only after Philippe Cousteau, son of the eminent undersea explorer Jacques Cousteau, visited Chuuk with his father in 1969 and produced the first major film on the shipwrecks, *Lagoon of the Lost Ships*, that world interest in them was aroused. Articles began appearing soon afterward in skin-diving magazines reporting on a new and exciting site for sport divers (Clark Graham interview).

Not long after Cousteau's visit, another famous diver led an expedition to Chuuk. Al Giddings, the renowned underwater photographer, brought a film crew to Truk

Table 1. Visitors, Chuuk and the FSM

	Chuuk	Total FSM
1969		20,600
1971	2,594	30,585
1972	2,909	36,199
1973	3,278	47,115
1974	3,820	60,835
1975	3,861	66,017
1976	3,965	18,697
1977	4,801	22,230
1978	5,749	23,111
1979	6,110	27,311
1981	6,631	15,948
1987	5,060	14,470
1996	3,532	18,305
1997	5,578	17,359

Table 1 continued

	Chuuk	Total FSM
1998	4,094	14,526
1999	5,112	15,367
2000	6,857	19,497
2001	4,256	15,884
2002	6,066	18,480
2003	5,599	18,762
2004	6,291	18,581
2005	5,586	18,954
2006	6,004	19,276
2007	7,197	21,015
2008	7,051	21,600
2009	6,569	20,567
2010	5,736	20,580
2011	5,092	18,986
2012	5,371	19,315
2013	6,375	20,141
2014	7,287	20,320
2015	5,570	17,059

Notes:
FSM figures for 1971–1975 are for the entire Trust Territory, including Saipan, Palau, and the Marshall Islands.
FSM figures for 1976–1978 include Palau and the Marshall Islands, then still part of the Trust Territory.
Figures for 1980–1986 and 1988–1995 are unavailable.

Sources:
1969 figure from TT 1969, 1.
1971–1978 figures from US Annual Reports on Trust Territory.
1979 figures from Hezel 1984: 44.
1981 figures from Pacific Daily News, Tourism Supplement, June 5, 1982.
1987 figures from Pollard 1989.
1996–2007 figures from Sturton 2009: Tables 6a and 6b (Note: these figures are for the fiscal year rather than calendar year).
2008–2013 figures for FSM (col B) from Chuuk Visitors Bureau data, Table 3a (includes FSM citizens and foreigners) (figures for the calendar year).
2008–2013 figures for Chuuk include those marked "Business and Employment" as well as "Visitors and Tourists." From Chuuk Visitors Bureau data, Table 3d.
2014 figures for FSM and Chuuk from Sturton 2015: Appendices, Tables 6a and 6b.

to search for the mysterious submarine sunk with all hands in April 1944 but never located. Giddings not only found the submarine, but he gave an enormous publicity boost to Truk. The film he produced on the search for the I-169, like Cousteau's earlier film, brought Truk lagoon to the attention of the American diving community (Hezel and Graham 1997, 1).

Other writers and filmmakers soon followed to record the marvels of Chuuk's underwater sites. Meanwhile, "teams of Japanese bone-collectors have come to reclaim the remains of their war dead and pay them the last honors they never received when they went down with their ships" (Hezel and Graham 1997, 2). In 1971, the Chuuk State Legislature formally declared the ships an underwater museum and forbade the removal of artifacts.

The first commercial dive shops appeared in the early 1970s. In 1973, Kimuio Aisek, a Chuukese from Tonoas who had made friends among the Japanese military and had lived through the wartime bombings, opened a dive shop known as the Blue Lagoon close to one of the smaller docks in town. In 1975, a former Peace Corps volunteer who had married a Chuukese woman started a second dive shop that he named Micronesian Aquatics. Before long, both were operating virtually side by side, close to the Continental Hotel (Bill Stinnett interview). The diving industry might have originally been located in town, but soon shifted out to the site of the Continental for a number of reasons. The move offered the dive shops proximity to the hotel, still the only major tourist facility in Chuuk, and its well-built dock. Additionally, the hotel, removed as it was from the town and protected by guards, provided distance and security from the wild drinking behavior that was becoming a notable problem throughout Chuuk at this time.

Chuuk, in short, had everything that was thought to be needed for a growing tourism industry: improved plane service and superb promotional work by the carrier, a quality tourist hotel situated near dive shops, and an asset in the Japanese sunken fleet that had become internationally renowned. Yet, the visitor figures for the 1970s are unremarkable (Table 1). Although the number of visitors gradually doubled during the 1970s—from 2,594 to 5,749—there were none of the sharp upward spikes normally associated with the sudden takeoff of a tourist destination. Wreck divers, lured by the undersea wonders of the Japanese ships, had found their way to Chuuk, but their numbers were too small to ground an industry that would reshape the local economy. Perhaps wreck diving was too tiny a market on which to base such hopes.

Dive pioneer Kimiuo Aisek may have foreseen this; he used to say that the shipwrecks would someday rust out and collapse, leaving no reason for divers to visit the lagoon and so rendering his crew at Blue Lagoon jobless. Farsightedly, from the late 1980s through the early 2000s, he had his crews explore shark-filled passes and outer island drop-offs with walls for dive sites that would compete with popular Palau. They tried to find manta ray cleaning stations like those found in Yap and Palau, current-fed points like Palau's famous Blue Corner, and beautiful walls like those in southern Palau. With his dive crews, he sent photojournalists Tim Rock of Guam, who wrote for Asian and American dive magazines, and Klaus Lindemann of Jakarta, who wrote for German magazines, to get exposure for the new sites. *Aquaquest Micronesia*, a TV series for which Rock was a producer, also did a series of programs depicting the "other side of Truk." Rock also produced a Lonely Planet diving and snorkeling guide book that featured many of these new sites.[5]

In the end, however, the shipwrecks overshadowed the natural reefs for a number of reasons. The wrecks had become adorned in beautiful soft corals and had an exquisite amount of reef life. Many divers were happy just to go to a wreck to see the fish and lush soft corals that were uncommon in other Micronesia dive destinations. The reef sites required long boat rides of an hour or more to the outer lagoon passes. Moreover, the guides had grown up on wrecks and were not familiar with what reef and wall divers wanted to see. While they could penetrate a pitch black engine room and not kick up a wisp of silt, they were not familiar with how to conduct a drift dive along a wall and sometimes they seemed more afraid of sharks than the

Chuuk had everything thought to be needed for a growing tourism industry.... Yet the the visitor figures for the 1970s are unremarkable

guests. Chuuk may have had some remarkable diving sites, but there was not a single site that had it all like Palau's Blue Corner.[6]

LATER TOURISM DEVELOPMENT IN CHUUK

Despite the stagnation of the tourism industry, a few new hotels continued to be built. Ray Setik, a prominent businessman and elected official, put up the 31-room Christopher Inn above the new supermarket he opened in 1971. During the 20 years the hotel was in operation, its clientele were mainly government travelers and businessmen, although a few European wreck divers were among its guests during its early years (Vicky Setik interview). Today, the building is gutted and abandoned, another eyesore in a town filled with such shells of failed business attempts.

Another hotel opened in the mid-1980s under the name of Chuuk Star. A local entrepreneur who had retired from the police force, Oshiro Billimon, was granted a loan from the FSM Development Bank to build this 29-room hotel in the hope of capturing the long-awaited tourist boom when it finally occurred. (The FSM Development Bank, following the pattern of the Economic Development Loan Fund in Trust Territory days, made generous sums of money available to Micronesian businessmen to encourage local investment in businesses.) From the very onset, though, the operation was financially shaky, and the owner was forced to sell the hotel when he had trouble repaying the original loan (Bill Stinnett interview).

For every hotel actually built, there were probably three or four that never got further than the planning stage. Each of the 12 major islands in the lagoon, and probably a few in the outer atolls as well, had visions of putting up a hotel to claim a share in the supposedly lucrative tourism industry. One high government official with family land on one of the islands on the western side of the lagoon proposed setting up a luxury hotel and golf course near a beautiful beach area on the island. But his dream, like so many others, remained unrealized (Kane Faylim interview).

> The law required local ownership or interest in a business for any new commercial venture.... Yet local investments had produced dubious results so far

At least two new dive shops, both owned by Chuukese, also went up during these years, but both were short-lived. In the early 1980s Pasi Eram started a dive shop near the Continental Hotel that survived for only a few years. Around the same time, Mark Mailo began a dive shop of his own in partnership with a Japanese man who was once married to a Chuukese woman and had been living on the island for years. Mailo's dive shop boasted a new high-tech dive boat that reportedly sold for a quarter of a million dollars. This operation, too, eventually failed, and the owners were forced to sell their assets. Neither of the dive shops was able to rival the clientele that Kimiuo Aisek's and Clark Graham's businesses had built (Bill Stinnett interview).

As local businessmen attempted to land a share of the stalled tourist industry in Chuuk, foreign companies began introducing a new twist in the trade: the live-aboard dive ship. When the first of several such vessels, the *Thorfinn*, applied for its business license in 1986, a crowd gathered around the Chuuk Legislature building to protest the application. Some of the pioneer divers objected to a newcomer entering the market after they had done years of work in finding and identifying the many shipwrecks in Chuuk. According to the law at that time, some local ownership or interest in the business was a requirement for any new commercial venture. Local people should derive some profit from business done in their islands—so the people argued and so the statutes stated. Yet, local investment had produced dubious results thus far.

When the matter was taken to the FSM National Government in Pohnpei, the *Thorfinn* was granted its business license a day or two later (Clark Graham and Bill Stinnett interviews).

Soon afterward, the *Thorfinn* began operations. Typically it would take on its dozen or so passengers shortly after they had landed at the Chuuk airport and whisk them off for a week of diving and relaxation aboard the vessel, discharging them the evening before they were to catch their plane home. Benefits to the local community were negligible in this brand of tourism since the guests spent virtually nothing on meals or lodging or even souvenirs. On the other hand, the rough condition of the roads, safety concerns, and other such issues were unlikely to discourage tourists who had booked on a live-aboard dive boat.

In the following years, other dive ships began servicing Chuuk. One of the best known was the *Truk Aggressor*, which left Chuuk about a decade ago. Probably the most popular is the *Odyssey*, which was once reportedly booked solid for a two-year stretch and is still serving the area. The newest of such ships is the *Siren*, which only began operating in the late summer of 2014.[7]

The live-aboard dive ships can each generally accommodate a few hundred tourists a year. Their clientele is small, even when measured against Chuuk's modest visitor totals. One owner of a land-based dive shop says that he does not view live-aboards as competing with the ordinary hotels and dive shops in Chuuk. These dive boats have their own small clientele, he claims. Such people normally shop around for a ship that appeals to them regardless of the part of the world in which it is operating (Bill Stinnett interview).

THE TRAPPINGS OF TOURISM TODAY

Today the dive industry is centered around two hotels: the Blue Lagoon and the Truk Stop, each with its own dive shop attached.

Blue Lagoon, formerly the Continental Hotel, was purchased by Kimiuo Aisek's family in 1998 as the airline sold off the remaining hotels it owned in the region. The Aisek family bought the hotel, now expanded to 54 rooms, and operated it along with a dive shop as part of a business package. In recent years, the hotel has catered mainly to recreational divers rather than wreck divers. Visitors are often brought to one of the two small islands owned by the Aisek family—Jeep Island and Kimiuo Orora Island—where they can live in rough cabins for up to a week. Jeep is very popular with Japanese tourists who do reef diving, snorkel, and search for dolphins in the summer time. There is also a World War II museum on the hotel grounds that was built as a memorial to Kimiuo Aisek, the deceased head of the family and the pioneer of undersea diving in Chuuk.

Truk Stop, located just outside the port town, was opened in 1993 by Bill and Kiki Stinnett. From the start, the 21-room hotel served mainly divers, although some government visitors and businessmen would stay there, especially after the road from town to the Continental worsened. In order to compete with Blue Lagoon, the Stinnetts were obliged to set up a dive shop of their own as part of the hotel operation. Although most of their clientele were general divers at first, the hotel soon began attracting a more specialized subgroup: deep divers who were prepared to go down to greater depths and stay there much longer. These technical divers included some Americans, but mostly consisted of Italians, Germans, Russians, and other Europeans. To serve the needs of this specialized group, the owners had to import nitrogen

Benefits to the local community from live-aboard dive ships are negligible; on the other hand, Chuuk's rough roads and safety issues don't discourage these visitors

and helium to be used in the rebreathing units that recycled the divers' own air much like a submarine (Bill Stinnett interview).[8]

The diving industry is also served by an independent dive shop (Truk Ocean Service) run by the long-time Japanese resident who once had partnered with Mark Mailo in his business. In addition, there are currently two dive ships operating in Chuuk: *Thorfinn* and *Odyssey*.

The other hotels on the island, including one just finished in late 2014, serve government and business travelers and those few tourists who have no interest in diving. All are modest-sized and owned by Chuukese. The Pacific Garden, a 10-room hotel located at the end of the airport runway, was built by Kachutosy Paulus sometime during the 1990s and is still in operation. The High Tide, formerly known as the Chuuk Star, was bought by Mitasy Aisek in the early 1990s and is operating alongside a popular restaurant belonging to the same owner. The 10 apartments in the Kurassa, which takes its name from its location across from the rock crusher, double as rental units for residents when not serving as hotel rooms. The building was opened about 10 years ago by the Mori family. Another of the Mori family, P.J. Mori, is the owner of the Runway, a 10-room hotel situated above the Leiside Restaurant close to the airport.

Perhaps the most ambitious of all the new hotels is the one known simply as L5. The five-story building that houses this hotel was built by Raymond Setik as the RS Plaza, but some years later Kembo Mida purchased the property and the building, made extensive renovations, and opened the building as a combined hotel-apartment-office building. Beside the 12 hotel rooms, there are four apartments rented out on a monthly or yearly basis, as well as several offices that are rented out to government departments. The owner is not interested in breaking into the diver-tourist market, he claims; instead, he sees his hotel as serving middle- or high-end government travelers (Kembo Mida interview).

GAUGING CHUUK TOURISM

Over the course of some 40 years, the number of visitors to Chuuk has grown from about 3,000 in 1972 to a little more than double that number (6,302) in 2014 (Table 1). Most of that growth, however, occurred during the 1970s, the early years of Chuuk's ascendency as a world-famous wreck-diving site. In 1978, the last year for which we have reliable figures, Chuuk's visitors numbered 5,749 (Table 1). Since that year, the number of visitors has shown almost no growth. Hence, the tourist boom that was expected in Chuuk with its sudden rise to fame as a wreck-diving site was short-lived and modest.[9]

The breakdown of the nationality of visitors in 2014 reveals that 40 percent are from the United States; another 20 percent are from Japan; and the remainder is divided among those from Australia, Europe, and a smattering of other countries (Sturton 2015, Appendices, Table 6b).

As we might imagine, the tourism industry on Chuuk has had a discouragingly small impact on the local economy. As reported in the FSM Economic Review for FY2012, restaurants and hotels (used as a rough measure of tourism dollars in the local economy) accounted for just 1.5 percent of the total Chuuk economy—$0.9 million out of a total Chuuk GDP of $66.8 million (Sturton 2014a, Table 2a).

The tourism industry, once regarded as the prospective engine of an island economy that is without other sources of revenue, has failed to live up to these hopes. Chuuk's economy, like that of the entire FSM, has shown no increase whatsoever over the past several years (Sturton

The tourism industry, once regarded as the prospective engine of an island economy that is without other sources of revenue, has failed to live up to these hopes

2014a, Table 1a). In view of this stall in economic growth, many Chuukese have been leaving home to find overseas employment opportunities they cannot find at home. In recent years, this has meant that Chuuk has experienced a loss of about 2,400 of its citizens a year—or close to 5 percent of its resident population—even as it welcomes 5,000 or 6,000 visitors yearly.[10] This emigration is as much a testimony to the dashed hopes of a prosperous tourism industry as the low visitor numbers themselves.

TOURISM: THE NATIONAL PICTURE

Chuukese emigration is as much a testimony to the dashed hopes of a prosperous tourism industry as the low visitor numbers themselves

The data for the entire nation suggest that Chuuk's tourist problem was not peculiar to this state. If the number of visitors in Chuuk showed little increase over the years, the whole of the FSM showed even less. Indeed, the total number of visitors for the FSM dropped from 23,111 in 1978 to 20,320 in 2014. During this same period, as we have seen, the yearly visitor count for Chuuk grew slightly from 5,749 to 6,302 (Table 1). Even during the more recent period (2008–2014) over which Chuuk visitors dropped by 750, the entire FSM lost nearly twice that number. This suggests, of course, that the factors responsible for the stagnation of the tourist industry in Chuuk were shared by the nation.

Likewise, the distribution of visitors by nationality in the FSM follows a similar pattern to what we have seen in Chuuk. Of all FSM visitors in 2014, 40 percent were from the United States, 17 percent were from Japan, and 13 percent were European (Sturton 2015, Appendices, Tables 6a & 6b). It may be worth noting that the tourism industry in the FSM, like that in Chuuk, has become less concentrated on one or two countries than it was in 1985, when 60 percent of the visitors were from the United States and 25 percent from Japan (Pollard 1989, 2). Clearly, despite Chuuk's niche market of wreck-diving enthusiasts, the distribution of visitors by nationality does not differ significantly from that of the FSM as a whole.

The states of Yap and Kosrae are both harder to reach than Chuuk or Pohnpei because fewer weekly flights serve these islands. Unsurprisingly, their visitor numbers for 2014 are well below the yearly total for Chuuk, with 4,361 for Yap and 1,307 for Kosrae (Sturton 2015, Appendices, Tables 6c & 6e). Pohnpei, the capital of the FSM, shows a considerably larger number of visitors if we count those who come for business and employment as well as tourists: in 2014, 8,350 for Pohnpei compared with 6,302 for Chuuk (Sturton 2015, Appendices, Tables 6b & 6d). When we count only those labeled as "visitors and tourists," however, Chuuk leads Pohnpei 5,524 to 4,869. Hence, Chuuk's tourism industry, as underdeveloped as it might be, is still the strongest of any of the states in the FSM.

Although tourism was marked as one of the three major pillars of the economy in the FSM's early development plans (the other two were agriculture and fishing), the contribution of tourism to the FSM economy has been minimal (FSM 1992). In 2013, the contribution of restaurants and hotels (a surrogate measure of tourism) to the FSM Gross Domestic Product, which was valued at $289 million, was only $5.4 million (Sturton 2014a, Table 1f). This constitutes a mere 2 percent of the total economy, with manufacturing measuring lower (Sturton 2014a, 15). Indeed, if inflation is taken into account, the contribution of tourism to the economy would have dropped in those 10 years from $6.8 million to $5.4 million in constant 2014 dollars.

The absence of growth in an industry that was expected to propel the FSM economy is especially distressing at this critical time. The 20-year funding period that began when the

Compact of Free Association was amended in 2003 is quickly running out, and the United States has repeatedly indicated it has no plans to continue its support for the FSM after 2023. With the national accounts showing a reduction of 2.9 percent a year since the start of the amended Compact, an economic boost is badly needed. Thus, the words of the *FSM 2012 Economic Review* ring true: "It is clear that the performance of the (tourism) sector has been lackluster and well below the potential for an industry designated as *a*—if not *the*—major growth sector of the FSM economy" (Sturton 2014a, 16).

.

FUTURE PROMISE AND CHALLENGE

Can tourism grow in the FSM? It would certainly seem so. The natural beauty of the island nation, Chuuk in particular, is no less appealing than, say, Fiji and Vanuatu—two Pacific countries that have become very popular tourist destinations in recent years. Sport diving in Chuuk could expand as it has in Palau, and perhaps even the more limited market for wreck diving could be more successfully tapped, if only . . .

And here the discussion of the obstacles to tourist development begins.

"Growth in demand is hampered by reliance on a single carrier (United Airlines) operating high priced flights," stated a recent economic review of the FSM (Sturton 2014a,17). This echoes an old complaint about the inadequate and expensive air service to the islands. Years ago, in an article in *Guam Business*, an official for Continental Airlines (later to merge with United Airlines) was quoted as protesting that flights from Guam to the FSM at that time averaged only 42 percent of passenger capacity, 16 percent below what is needed to make a profit (Campbell 1998). His implicit argument was that if Continental, which had already engaged in an ambitious marketing program on behalf of the islands for 20 years, could not come close to filling its planes, why would the airline add still more flights and bring down prices at the same time. What comes first—the air service or the tourist demand for it? In the case of Palau, clearly the number of flights was ratcheted up as the demand grew.

Then there is the issue of substandard tourist facilities. "Hotel facilities offer a standard of accommodation unattractive to international travelers," an economic report pointed out in its attempt to identify the constraints to tourism growth in the FSM (Sturton 2014a, 17). Yet, Chuuk had a four-star hotel (Continental Hotel), well-maintained and situated near a beautiful beach, along with a fine restaurant for nearly 30 years. The luxury hotel might have been a welcome feature for those visitors who came to Chuuk during its operation, but it was insufficient to grow the tourism industry even to the point that another such hotel might profitably be built.

One writer, citing a public document, noted that the depressing conditions in Chuuk played a role in the lack of tourist growth. Weno, the document claimed, was "severely hampering the reputation and development of tourism in the FSM. Visitors complain about safety and security, unfriendly residents, the wholly inadequate infrastructure (poor airport conditions, poor roads, unsafe drinking water, unreliable water and electricity), defacing and vandalism of the historic items and sites" (Campbell 1998). The long list of problems is undeniably accurate. But are these conditions really to blame for the nongrowth of tourism? If so, what would explain the similar lack of tourist growth in places like Pohnpei and Yap, where conditions are better than in Chuuk?

Other obstacles to tourism development frequently cited in economic reports include the difficulty of obtaining secure land for tourist facilities and the problems often encountered by foreign investors who are considering a business venture in the FSM. "According to the World Bank 'Doing Business Survey,' the FSM ranks 150th out of a total of 185 nations surveyed," states one such report (Sturton 2014a, 17). The report goes on to call for the reforms needed to achieve an attractive climate for investment in the islands. The problem of obtaining secure long-term land leases was highlighted two years ago in Pohnpei when The Village, a successful high-end hotel, was forced to go out of business after landowners refused to extend the original lease. This sort of problem has plagued Chuuk even more frequently, with many public facilities being shut down by landowners who insisted on higher lease payments. Yet, oddly enough, tourist facilities in Chuuk have not had many such problems. Almost all the hotels there have been locally owned and built on family land. The one notable exception was the Continental Hotel, but the hotel never seemed to experience any such difficulty in the course of its 20 years of operation. Palauans, too, seem to have been able to navigate around this difficulty, as they have the problem of securing business licenses for foreign investors, even though both issues were once as problematic there as anywhere else in Micronesia. The ease with which the live-aboard dive ships secured their business permits suggests that the difficulty is anything but insuperable.

CONCLUSIONS

The historical view of tourism in the FSM, mostly through the lens of the ups and downs of the industry in Chuuk State, may not offer a ready formula for growing tourism, but it can suggest a few lessons on the subject. This final section offers a few lessons learned from comparing the FSM with Palau.

Palau, with its now-successful tourist industry of 150,000 visitors yearly, developed from the same slender base as Chuuk and the rest of the FSM. Indeed, after the construction of the new Continental Hotel hotels in Palau and Chuuk in 1970, Chuuk seemed to offer more promise of becoming a major tourist attraction, thanks to the wreck diving there that received sudden attention.

Palau faced many of the same constraints as Chuuk, but was able to overcome these. The obstacles to foreign investment were disposed of, one piece at a time, in response to real opportunities. It was encounters with businessmen, who worked closely with local business and government leaders, that worked this magic in Palau. When there are real business opportunities at stake, legal problems can be solved easily.

Sport or recreational diving might not be attractive to everyone, but it provides a broad enough base for tourism to lure others—even those who are not especially interested in diving —to a destination. Wreck diving, on the other hand, seems to have strong appeal for only a relatively small number of visitors, especially from Asia. Wreck diving is not a strong foundation on which to build a booming tourism industry, although sport diving may well be. Palau, for example, is said to have more World War II shipwrecks than Chuuk. Most are located quite close to Koror and are in sheltered areas where they can be explored on a consistent basis. Yet, these wrecks are seldom visited and are considered no more than a novelty in the Palau diving world.[11]

The FSM's location well to the east of Palau and with no direct access to Asia is a serious drawback for the development of tourism there. Apart from the longer flying time and the higher airfare prices, visitors cannot easily continue their tour of the area and are forced to

A dead-end destination creates a marketing problem for a locale that is already distant

double back to Guam. A dead-end destination creates a marketing problem for a locale that is already distant.

Local conditions ought to be kept in perspective where tourism is concerned. Despite the well-publicized problems in Chuuk (e.g., bad roads, poor infrastructure, government mismanagement), its tourist numbers are comparable to other states in the FSM, suggesting that the unique problems in Chuuk have had little notable impact on its tourism. Chuuk's visitor figures are currently higher than Pohnpei and the other states of the FSM, as already noted.

There is little evidence that the growth of tourism is due chiefly to the successful implementation of institutional reforms. While such reforms may be desirable, they are often brought about in response to the demand of a growing tourism industry. In asking what brings about the initial demand and how that demand can be sustained, we may be dealing with elements of chance—visits and relationships that somehow manage to tip the balance.

REFERENCES

Publications

Ames, Todd. 2011. "Socio-Economic Development in Micronesia: A Case Study of Hope and Heartbreak in Chuuk, FSM." *Pacific Asia Inquiry* vol 2:1, 195–203.

Campbell, Bruce. 1998. "Palm Trees and Concrete: Tourism in the FSM." *Guam Business News*. June.

Chuuk Visitors Bureau. 2015. Visitors to Chuuk and FSM, 2008–2013. Digital file with tables by state and year. Chuuk, Federated States of Micronesia.

CVB. *See* Chuuk Visitors Bureau.

Federated States of Micronesia. 1992. *Federated States of Micronesia: Second National Development Plan, 1992–1996*. Palikir, Pohnpei: FSM Office of Planning & Statistics.

FSM. *See* Federated States of Micronesia.

Hezel, Francis X. 1984. "A Brief Economic History of Micronesia" in *Past Achievements and Future Possibilities: A Conference on Economic Development, Pohnpei, May 22–25*. Micronesian Seminar. www.micsem.org/pubs/articles/economic/frames/ecohistfr.htm.

———. 1995. *Strangers in Their Own Land: A Century of Colonial Rule in the Caroline and Marshall Islands*. Pacific Islands Monograph Series, no. 13. Honolulu: University of Hawai'i Press.

Hezel, Francis X., and Clark Graham. 1997. *Truk Underwater Museum: A Report on the Sunken Japanese Ships, Federated States of Micronesia*. San Francisco: Micronesian Endowment for Historic Preservation, Federated States of Micronesia, US National Park Service.

Pollard, Steve. 1989. "Tourism in the Federated States of Micronesia." Working Paper 9 for the Federated States of Micronesia Second National Development Plan 1990–1994. Pohnpei: FSM National Government, Office of Planning and Statistics.

Rock, Tim. 2000. *Diving & Snorkeling Chuuk Lagoon, Pohnpei & Kosrae*. Australia: Lonely Planet Publications.

Sturton, Mark. 2006. *Federated States of Micronesia FY2005 Economic Review*. Pohnpei: FSM National Government. June. www.pitiviti.org/news/wp-content/uploads/FSM/FSM_EconReview_FY05.pdf.

———. 2009. *Federated States of Micronesia Fiscal Year 2008 Economic Review*. Honolulu: Graduate School USA, PITI-VITI. August. www.pitiviti.org/news/wp-content/uploads/FSM/FSM_EconReview_FY08_wStats.pdf.

———. 2014a. *Federated States of Micronesia Fiscal Year 2012 Economic Review*. 2 Vols: Report and Statistical Appendices. Honolulu: Graduate School USA, PITI-VITI. February.

www.pitiviti.org/news/wp-content/uploads/downloads/2014/02/FSM_EconReview_FY12.pdf.

———. 2014b. *Federated States of Micronesia Fiscal Year 2012 Economic Review*. 2 Vols: Report and Statistical Appendices. Honolulu: Graduate School USA, PITI-VITI. August.

www.pitiviti.org/news/wp-content/uploads/downloads/2014/02/FSM_EconReview_FY12.pdf

———. 2015. *Federated States of Micronesia Fiscal Year 2014 Economic Review*. Report and Statistical Appendices. Graduate School USA, PITI-VITI, Honolulu. August.

www.pitiviti.org/news/wp-content/uploads/downloads/2015/10/FSM_EconReview_FY14_Final Web.pdf.

Trust Territory Government. 1969. "Tourism Status Report for the Year January–December 1969." Saipan: Department of Resources and Development.

———. 1970. "Travel Information." Saipan: Department of Resources and Development. January.

TT. *See* Trust Territory Government.

US Department of State. 1969–1978. *Annual Report on the Administration of the Trust Territory of the Pacific Islands*. Washington, DC: Government Printing Office.

Interviews

Kane Faylim	Manager, Chuuk International Airport
Clark Graham	Former diveshop owner
Kembo Mida	Owner, L5 Hotel
Vicky Setik	Daughter of Raymond Setik
Bill and Kiki Stinnett	Owners, Truk Stop Hotel

NOTES

[1] For more information on the secession movement and the adoption of the FSM constitution as a compromise document, see Hezel 1995: 345–357.

[2] Saipan's two hotels were the Hafa Adai and the Saipan Hotel, both built by local businessmen. At this time Tinian and Rota had their own small hotels as well.

[3] Visitor figures are taken from the US State Department's *Annual Report on the Administration of the Trust Territory of the Pacific Islands* for those years.

[4] Continental originally intended to build six hotels to be managed by TraveLodge, but only four (including the Continental Hotel on Guam) were actually built. The proposed hotels for Pohnpei and Yap met with local resistance and so were dropped.

[5] Tim Rock generously provided this detail on the futile attempts of local dive masters to broaden the scope of Chuuk's tourist base. For his publication on Chuuk diving, see Rock 2000.

[6] For this assessment I am indebted to Tim Rock, personal communication, August 21, 2015. Rock, a well-known underwater photographer with long experience in the area, added a final comment on the subject. "As Kimiuo got older and was not as often present in the dive scene, the dive operations and dive masters gravitated back to doing almost entirely shipwreck diving. Only the *Odyssey* now makes a regular outer reef pass shark dive as part of its weekly agenda."

[7] Both the *Odyssey* and *Truk Siren* were damaged in a March 2015 typhoon. The *Odyssey* went back into service in August 2015. The *Siren*'s fate is still not known.

[8] Tim Rock notes that this tiny niche of an already small niche has begun to catch on in Chuuk. "Now Blue Lagoon Diveshop and the *Odyssey* also cater to technical and rebreather divers as the tech diving industry gains in popularity and safety" (Rock, personal communication, August 21, 2015).

[9] The figures for 2008–2013 obtained from the Chuuk Visitors Bureau show the total number of arrivals at between 8,500 and 9,400 during these years. But when seamen and prospective employees are subtracted, visitor numbers range from 6,400 to 5,600 during this period (CVB 2015, Table 3d).

[10] Departure rates are taken from the net loss in air passage recorded by the Division of Immigration and Labor, FSM Department of Justice. These data may be found in CVB 2015, Table 1a. The estimated emigration from Chuuk is consistent with figures derived from other sources.

[11] Tim Rock (personal communication, August 21, 2015) offered this interesting comparison between Chuuk and Palau.

Tourism in Palau

PALAU'S TOURISM TODAY

Visitors to Palau can now enter the island group on any of the 33 flights a week offered by various airlines serving the small nation: United Airlines (from Guam or Manila), Japan Airlines or Delta Airlines (from Tokyo), China Airlines or Trans Asia Airways (from Taipei), Asian Air (from Macau), Asiana Airlines or Korean Air (from Seoul), Dynamic Airways or Mega Global Maldives (from Hong Kong), or Palau Pacific Airways (from different cities in China). As arriving passengers leave the airport and head for town, they cross the Koror-Babeldaob Bridge over the deepwater channel dividing Babeldaob from Koror, the port town and population center of the island group. They can check into any of 40 hotels, ranging from the five-star Palau Pacific Resort—the first of the real luxury hotels—to one of the smaller, locally owned budget hotels. Altogether Palau has a total of over 1,600 rooms, 500 of which are found in its five world-class resorts: Palau Pacific Resort, Palasia Hotel, Palau Plantation Resort, Sea Passion Hotel, and Papago International Resort.

Increasingly, visitors come to Palau to explore underwater seascapes. If diving is their goal, there are numerous dive shops and diving services, including MAML Divers, Neco Marine, Fish 'n Fins, Sam's Tours, Antelope, Aqua Magic, Big Blue Explorer, Cruise Control, Carp Island Resort, Paradise Divers, Peleliu Divers, Southern Marine Divers, UBDI Blue Marlin, Palau Aggressor II, Day Dreams, Pacific Divers Oasis, and Palau Dive Adventures. Divers can go out by the day or get a room on a live-aboard dive ship like the *Aggressor*. They can dive

The Rock Islands in Palau. *Photograph by Tim Rock.*

off sunken wrecks from World War II or explore the walls of the reef and enjoy the countless species of marine life. Sightseeing is also a favorite, combined with picnicking and diving, at the famous Rock Islands, the mushroom-shaped coral islets that lie just off the tip of Koror. In the middle of these islands, Jellyfish Lake once teemed with hundreds of thousands of the luminous golden creatures. Now their number has dramatically declined; why is not known. Everyone is hoping for a rebound.

For the less adventurous who want to confine their exploration to above-water pursuits, there is a choice of tour companies: Peleliu Adventures, Ocean Hunter II, Pleasure Island Palau, Dildoseb eco Tours, IMPAC Tours, or Palau Rock Island Tour Company. World War II buffs can turn to Peleliu Adventures if they want to visit Peleliu, the island that was the site of one of the bloodiest Pacific battles. A few companies also specialize in eco tours, and some cruise operators, such as Seabird Luxury Cruise, cater to those who prefer sightseeing in comfort. Tourists wishing to get around the islands in other ways can choose Palau Bikers, Palau Helicopters, and Ungil Sils Water Taxi.

What else is there to see in Palau? Cultural sites include the ancient terraces and monoliths in Babeldaob. And there are two cultural museums—Belau National Museum and the privately owned Etpison Museum—as well as the World War II Memorial Museum on Peleliu. Nature lovers can visit the freshwater Lake Ngardok Nature Reserve in Melekeok, or they can see salt-water crocodiles, manta rays, sharks, and other marine creatures—either in their natural habitat or at the Palau Aquarium at the Palau International Coral Reef Center. And for a bird's-eye view, the more daring tourists can savor the excitement of riding the zip-line that soars over the Taki Waterfall Park at the northern end of Babeldaob.

For such a small getaway, Palau offers a broad variety of attractions, many ways to enjoy them, and a fine selection of hotels to choose from. Not bad for an island group that, 50 years ago, had a single 12-room hotel, was serviced by one weekly flight from Guam, and was generally regarded as a lonely outpost at the edge of the US-administered Trust Territory of the Pacific Islands.

For such a small getaway, Palau offers a broad variety of attractions, many ways to enjoy them, and a fine selection of hotels to choose from

PALAU: BACKGROUND

Located in the North Pacific Ocean just above the equator, the Republic of Palau is a cluster of about 300 islands, only nine of which are inhabited, with a total land area of 196 square miles. Palau is about 800 miles southwest of Guam, 500 miles east of the Philippines, 1,400 miles from the northern tip of Australia, and 2,000 miles south of Tokyo. Seventy percent of Palau's 20,000 people reside in Koror, the country's commercial and administrative center and until recently its capital. The large island of Babeldaob to the north, about 20 miles long and home to a quarter of the country's population, is largely undeveloped.

Although self-governing since 1980, Palau attained formal independence and membership in the United Nations only in 1994. In that year the nation entered into the Compact of Free Association with the United States, finally terminating the administrative oversight that the United States had exercised over Palau since the end of World War II.

By 1980 Palau was well-prepared to face the challenges of self-government, even if its economy was as underdeveloped as the economies of the other island groups of Micronesia. An early attempt in the 1960s to build a fishing industry with the help of Van Camp Fisheries, coupled with a sideline of boatbuilding, had little effect in generating substantial gains for Palau's economy (Hezel 1995, 319–320). Exports from the mid-1960s through the next decade continued to consist of little more than scrap metal salvaged from the war, copra, and a modest supply of fish. Subsequent attempts to spark one industry after another produced no better results. The coconut-processing plant that was opened in 1977 to produce oil from the copra lasted only five years (Hezel 1984). Yet, some notable improvements in the infrastructure were made during this period, as the United States invested millions of dollars in the development of roads and airfields throughout Micronesia. By the early 1980s, Palau's main town of Koror had good paved roads for the first time. Moreover, the towering single-span bridge between Koror and Babeldaob, built with Japanese funding, had been dedicated in 1977. This opened up the large island of Babeldaob to Koror, just as the newly paved airstrip in Babeldaob, when it was finally completed in 1985, would open up the entire island group to the rest of the world.

Palau's most important resource was probably its educated population. Palau had modernized late by comparison with most of its Micronesian neighbors—Palauans were still garbed in traditional loincloths and grass skirts when other Caroline Islanders had already been introduced to school. But when the Germans and later the Japanese introduced a program of modernization in the early twentieth century, Palauans firmly embraced development and formal education. Fueled by the intense competitiveness that was such a key part of their culture, Palauans excelled in school and eagerly sought wage employment. Throughout Japanese rule and under US post-war administration, Palau moved from perhaps the most traditional island group to the most advanced. Despite their relatively small population, Palauans were notable for the number of scholarships they won and the key administrative positions they held in the Trust Territory government.

> Palau's most important resource was probably its educated population

Since the first years of US administration, Palauans had been leaving in small numbers each year to find better jobs abroad. The number of emigrants increased substantially in the early 1970s when Micronesians first became eligible for US federal education benefits. From 1972 to the present the local population in Palau has plateaued as hundreds left each year to study and work abroad. Given the thirst for education and jobs that had been characteristic of Palauans for so long, there was little chance that those who remained behind would settle for a life of fishing and farming rather than seize every opportunity for personal development (Hezel and Levin 1990, 42–44).

EARLY BEGINNINGS OF TOURISM

Back in the 1960s, the 12-room Royal Palauan Hotel was more than adequate for the few visitors to Palau, most of whom were on government business or were prospective employees. The arrival of Continental Airlines in 1968, however, brought a new enterprising spirit to the islands. Air Micronesia planned to extend its routes to Asia even as it constructed hotels on as many of the major islands as possible. By 1970 Continental had opened a new 50-room hotel on Palau along with the ones it put up on Guam, Saipan, and Chuuk. The Palau hotel, never more than modestly successful, was later sold to a Japanese firm and ran under the name Nikko Hotel until it was finally closed in 2001.

A couple more small hotels were started—the Palau Hotel and the Kinjo—each with just a few rooms. These hotels, like the new restaurants and bars that opened in the 1960s and

Table 1. Visitor Arrivals, Tourists, and Hotel Rooms by Year

Year	Visitors	Tourists	Hotel Rooms
1980	5,640	4,516	80
1981	5,057	3,902	
1982	5,330	3,995	
1983	6,388	4,449	
1984	9,014	6,129	
1985	13,371	10,740	
1986	13,653	10,349	
1987	16,695	11,834	
1988	22,675	16,453	
1989	26,005	19,394	
1990	32,846	23,398	
1991	32,700	23,769	
1992	36,117	28,033	
1993	40,497	32,125	573
1994	44,073	35,030	
1995	53,229	44,850	699
1996	69,330	58,020	709
1997	73,719	63,601	
1998	64,194	54,530	
1999	55,493	42,819	973
2000	57,732	45,411	991
2001	54,111	44,454	997
2002	58,560	50,513	1,049
2003	68,296	59,851	1,050
2004	94,895	83,041	1,253
2005	86,124	76,180	
2006	87,206	78,252	
2007	93,031	84,566	
2008	83,114	75,829	
2009	83,795	68,329	
2010	92,500	82,202	
2011	118,055	107,205	1,380
2012	124,117	115,629	
2013	114,000	101,546	
2014	146,867	139,029	1,636
2015	167,966	160,370	

Notes:
Visitors is the total number of people other than residents entering Palau; this includes those coming to study, seek employment, or engage in business.
Tourists is the number of those visitors who claim that their purpose is recreation or vacation.

Sources:
Visitors 1980–1989: Palau Planning and Statistics Office.
Visitors 1990–2015: Palau Visitors Authority (PVA).
Tourists 1980–2002: PVA files.
Tourists 2003–2015: PVA figures from files (employment and business visitors must be subtracted).
Hotel rooms 1980: Warner et al. 1979, pg. 9.
Hotel rooms, 1993, 1996, 2002: Bank of Hawai'i reports on Palau, BOH 1997, 2000, 2003.
Hotel rooms 2000–2003: PVA.
Hotel rooms 2003 and 2004: Sakuma 2007.
Hotel rooms 2011 and 2014: PVA.

1970s, survived because of the prosperity built on the wages of government employees, whose numbers and salaries grew (Hezel 1984, 37–39). Visitors to Palau were still very few, and real tourists were almost nonexistent at the time. Most visitors during those years were there on official business. Yet, from time to time small groups of Japanese—servicemen who had been stationed in Palau during the war or former residents during the Japanese prewar administration —visited the island (Minoru Ueki interview). That was the first hint of real tourism in Palau.

In 1979, the hotels in Palau had a total of 80 rooms with a 40 percent occupancy rate. Palauans, who probably wished to see an increase in the number of visitors, were guarded in their expectations. In an interview conducted on the subject by researchers at the University of Guam, most Palauans claimed they did not want to follow the path of intense tourism that Guam and Hawai'i had taken. Both of those places were awash in hotels—Hawai'i with four million tourists a year and Guam with nearly a million. The expressed goal of the economic development officer on Palau at that time was to achieve a visitor total equal to twice Palau's population—in other words, about 30,000 a year (Warner et al 1979, 10). Most Palauans hoped that tourism would be just one of a number of industries cultivated in the islands. The 5,000 annual visitor total Palau received during the early 1980s did not warrant higher expectations (Table 1).

Then, in 1982, Air Nauru inaugurated flights to Palau. The tiny Republic of Nauru, wealthy from the phosphate it was exporting, proudly sponsored a national airline of its own that was just beginning to map out new routes across the Pacific. The plane bypassed Guam since it did not have landing rights there and flew from Nauru through Pohnpei and Chuuk to Palau. In the same year Air Nauru opened a new route between Palau and Manila. That flight afforded Palau access to the Filipino foreign-worker market and permitted the entry of construction workers, domestic workers, and employees in the service industries. Within a year of the opening of the new route—even as Continental was in the process of beginning its own flight service—Palau's visitor-arrival data began to show 1,000 or more Asians a year coming for employment (PVA 1982). The hope that Manila would serve as a portal for wealthier Asians who might have wished to vacation in Palau never developed to the degree that planners anticipated. Even so, the flight marked a significant moment: For the first time Palau was no longer a dead end on an airline route. The nation's first air link with Asia had been forged.[1]

For the first time Palau was no longer a dead end on an airline route. The nation's first air link with Asia had been forged

TOURISM TAKES OFF

In 1985, a five-star resort opened its doors on one of Palau's private pristine beaches. Suddenly, word spread and, for the first time in its history, Palau needed to negotiate a substantial flow of tourists (Zolli and Healy 2012).

The beginning of commercial tourism in Palau can be dated from the opening of the 100-room Palau Pacific Resort in 1985. Today, more than three decades later, the resort is still the premier hotel in the island group. Even more importantly, the manner in which the hotel was planned and built remains the gold standard.

The Palau Pacific Resort was not put up quickly. Japanese investor Noboru Gotoh, president of the gigantic Tokyu Corporation, paid a visit to Palau in 1967 as a member of a UN inspection team. He was immediately impressed by the beauty and tourism potential of the island group. Soon afterward he began talks with Palauan landowners, but it was not until 15 years later that the arrangements were concluded and actual construction of the hotel began. Gotoh reportedly wanted to build his new resort where guests could watch the setting sun. When he had selected his beachside site, an idyllic spot in one of the more remote parts of Koror, he learned there were rival claimants for the property he hoped to lease. Gotoh had the good sense to avoid dealing directly with the landowners. Instead, he worked through a few key Palauans who had the influence needed to acquire the land he wanted. Inabo Katsumi, the sectional chief of the area in which the hotel was to be built, collaborated with the paramount chief of Koror, his clanmate, to acquire rights to much of the beachfront property.

Meanwhile, Ngirakl Etpison, who later became president of Palau, began working with Katsumi and another Palauan to acquire the small plots of land owned by private individuals. The three formed a local company to purchase the land needed for the resort with funds provided by the Japanese investors. Since land titles for most of the parcels had not been established in the courts, it stood to reason that land disputes would inevitably arise and cause further delays to the project unless the Palauan company adopted a different approach. As Etpison's family recalls, "each piece of land had to be bought several times from different people and clans to make sure there would not be any claims later on" (Etpison 2009, 206–207).

Palauans today applaud the patience of the Japanese in conducting such arrangements. They contrast it with the haste with which hotel construction has been done in more recent years. While the negotiations for the Palau Pacific Resort went on, Gotoh and his associates did not sit around idly. The Japanese corporation put up one of the early hotels on Tumon Bay in Guam—the New Tokyu—using a Palauan motif and featuring a traditional Palauan meetinghouse alongside it. The corporation had sufficient time to build another hotel in Bali while it waited for clearance to put up its resort in Palau. The Japanese investor not only had to gain rights to the land he wanted, but he had to negotiate the foreign-investment maze as one of the first tourist investors in the island group. By the time he had secured final approval for the resort, the Palauan company that owned the land needed to lease the project to Tokyu Corporation. Any uncertainty about future lease renewals was forestalled when Tokyu brought the two Palauans into the company that owned the hotel.[2]

Working through a handful of influential Palauans may have elevated the rental fee for the investor, but at least he did not have to worry about a multitude of discordant voices raising their own concerns. With the land needed for the hotel concentrated in the hands of Etpison and Katsumi, the necessary business licenses and permits for construction could be obtained much more easily. Gotoh, in turn, gave both of these men influential positions in the hotel and made them senior officials. As a result, the Japanese never had to worry about land-lease renewal (then a 25-year lease term), since a few influential Palauans had good reason to support the resort. As the hotel grew, so did the money and influence of Etpison and Katsumi. The start-

'Each piece of land had to be bought several times from different people and clans to make sure there would not be any claims later on'

up negotiations were lengthy, but the outcome was exemplary in maintaining a proper balance between the interests of all parties, foreign and local.[3]

Meanwhile, the new international airport in Airai was completed in 1985. A landing strip had first been opened there in 1966, and so passengers could then fly directly to Palau's main land mass rather than land on Angaur, an island 50 miles to the south of Koror. (Before the relocation of the airport, it took almost as long to make the 50-mile boat ride from Angaur to Koror as it did to fly from Guam to Palau.) For years, the airfield was unpaved and offered two old sheds that served in place of a passenger terminal. Finally, in the same year that the new resort opened, the landing strip was paved and a concrete building was erected as a terminal.

With the airport completed and the new hotel—the first of its kind in Palau—finally in place, the flow of visitors into Palau increased from 9,000 to 13,000 between 1984 and 1985. Both the airfield and the resort served notice that Palau was now positioned to become a tourist destination. Although Palau Pacific Resort was pricey, it boasted a high occupancy rate, with Japanese tourists occupying most of its rooms. During those early years, visitors to Palau remained overwhelmingly Japanese. Only during the 1990s did the clientele diversify—a reflection of what was happening to tourism in Palau.

> During those early years, visitors to Palau remained overwhelmingly Japanese; only during the 1990s did the clientele diversify

A DECADE OF RAPID GROWTH: 1985–1994

Following the opening of the Palau Pacific Resort in 1985, the nation saw a rapid rise in the number of visitors—from 13,000 to 32,000 by 1990. Most were Japanese tourists, many of them scuba divers.[4]

Hotel construction leapt once Palau had discovered its tourism potential. Several of these new hotels were built with foreign assistance. One was the Sunrise Villa, built on a bluff above Echang, just a mile or so from the Palau Pacific Resort. The hotel was later sold, renamed the Cliffside, and is operated today by the son of Ngirakl Etpison. A much smaller operation, Carolines Hotel, was located nearby in the section of town known as Meyungs. After the successful opening of the Palau Pacific Resort, Meyungs appears to be have been designated the target area for development of the tourist industry.

Other hotels were opened in downtown Koror during these years. The best known were business hotels: the Penthouse, built by the widow of former president Lazarus Salii in 1992, and the Palau Hotel, opened above a large retail store. Other facilities opened at that time were the Yuhi Motel, Lehns Motel, DW Motel, Guest House Motel, and Tree-D Motel.

Not all the hotels that were built during this period were entirely financed and owned by outside investors. The West Plaza hotels, now numbering five with a total of 130 rooms, sprang from WCTC—Western Carolines Trading Company, as it was once known. WCTC, a venerable store with a pedigree dating back to the early 1950s, had been run as a joint-stock company since its origin. It built the hotels in the same way that the company itself had been founded: through local investment and stock purchased by Palauans. From the time the hotels were put up through the present, ownership has remained in the hands of Palauans (Minoru Ueki interview).

Some of the hotels opened during the visitor boom of the early 1990s were unable to survive, and at least one ended in disaster. The Airai View, located not far from the airport in

Babeldaob, was an impressive 100-room hotel, nicely appointed and featuring an Olympic-size swimming pool. The Japanese-Korean businessman who had provided the funding for the construction was working with Roman Tmetuchl, a prominent political figure and business-man who owned the land on which the hotel was built. There had been problems between the investor and his local partner on the ownership and business arrangements right from the start, but these came to a head only after the construction was completed. The matter ended tragically when the investor, in despair of ever reaching a satisfactory agreement with his local partner, attempted to set fire to the hotel, doused himself with gasoline, and committed suicide.[5]

Then, in the early 1990s, a number of things happened that put Palau on the map. Palau first leaped to international fame in 1993 when the late John F. Kennedy, Jr. and American actress Daryl Hannah spent their diving holiday in this Pacific destination ordinarily far removed from the western paparazzi (Cagurangan and Peterson 2011). Even so, the publicity Palau received from their visit made no significant impact on tourism from the United States, as the visitor figures show in Table 1.

In 1994, Palau finally celebrated its formal independence, although it had been effectively self-governing in the previous 15 years. The celebration was attended by government officials and dignitaries from all over the Pacific, Western Asia, and Washington.

Just a few months after its independence party, Palau hosted the Festival of Pacific Arts. Because the event brought hundreds of visitors from all over the Pacific to the new island nation, visitor numbers surged that year.[6]

Throughout this period the number of Japanese visitors to the island grew steadily, tripling from 6,500 to 20,500. Not all these Japanese visitors were wealthy, but most tended to be at least mid-end tourists. At the same time, American tourists grew in number, most of them divers attracted to Palau's world-famous sites. By 1995, there were close to 10,000 visitors from the United States each year, half of whom could be called tourists. The handful of hotels a few years before had grown to 20, providing nearly 700 rooms. By this time there were already 38 tour companies, with 16 of them offering diving tours (US DOI 1995).

On top of all this, the next tourist boom in Palau was just beginning as the Taiwan market opened up.

START OF THE TAIWAN TOURIST TRADE

Visitors from Taiwan had started trickling into Palau as early as 1989, but it wasn't until 1994 that the numbers began to attract the serious attention of tourism planners. Continental Airlines, always looking for ways to expand its routes, had been planning to inaugurate a new flight between Guam and Taipei ever since 1990. As an added incentive to Taiwanese travelers, Continental began serious promotion of even more-distant Palau as a vacation spot. Why Palau and not one of the other island groups in Micronesia? According to the director of the Palau Visitors Authority at the time, the location of Palau was a major consideration: Palau was less than five hours flying time from Taiwan. Moreover, Palau already had a luxury resort capable of handling high-end guests and the facilities in place to move them to dive spots and other attractions there. Palau would not need to build from the ground level up to handle the tourists Continental hoped to fly there (Mary Ann Delemel interview).

In the early 1990s, a number of things happened that put Palau on the map

The first tourists came, a couple hundred a month, generally booking into the Palau Pacific Resort and other upscale hotels. Then, in 1994, Continental began a direct flight from Taipei to Koror, flying twice weekly, even as the airline intensified its campaign on behalf of Palauan tourism through TV programs and advertising. Continental handled all the promotional work for Palau, in effect opening up the Taiwan market for Palau once and for all.

Continental's inaugural flight happened to coincide with the formal independence of Palau. Accordingly, the president of Taiwan and several senior government officials flew into Palau on a private government jet at about the same time. There they were wined and dined by President Tosiwo Nakamura and were introduced to both the natural wonders of Palau and the intricacies of its political machinery. Not long afterward, at the invitation of Taiwan's leaders, Palau established formal diplomatic relations with the Republic of China, severing its previous formal ties with the People's Republic of China, in keeping with the latter's adamant One-China policy. In return, Palau began receiving generous foreign-aid funds from the Republic of China (Mary Ann Delemel interview).

The opening of Continental's direct-flight service from Taipei to Palau in 1994 might have been the start of it all, but it was Palau's willingness to allow charter flights out of Taiwan a year later that really kicked off the tourism boom. When Taiwan requested reciprocal flight service, Palau immediately agreed to permit Taiwan charter flights to land. Two airlines—Far-Eastern Air Transport and China Airlines—provided the charter services and the number of flights increased to four a week[7] (Levy 1999, 3). Before long, Continental Airlines found that it could not compete with the Taiwan-based carriers, and so it closed its own Taipei–Palau route.

Continental may have failed to expand its own service in the area, but its promotion of Palau in Taiwan led to lasting impact on Palau's tourism. Visitors from Taiwan rose from 6,000 in 1994 to 11,000 the following year, and then doubled to 23,000 in 1996. Thereafter the numbers have generally been 20,000 or 30,000 a year, reaching a high of 42,000 in 2004, with the Taiwan trade comprising anywhere between 20 and 35 percent of the total Palau market in any given year (Table 2).

In 1997, the 265-room, multi-story Palasia Hotel opened—a premium hotel that especially catered to visitors from Taipei. Built in downtown Koror on private land belonging to one of the more notable Palauan entrepreneurs, the hotel was to be part of the Outrigger chain, but Outrigger pulled out even before the hotel opened. The Palasia has gone on to become one of the top-tier hotels in Palau and remains popular with Taiwanese visitors even after the opening of several other hotels catering to the Taiwanese tourist market. With the start of additional charter flights from Taiwan in 2011, the hotel was registering an occupancy rate of 95 percent (Cagurangan and Peterson 2011).

'Tour packages are typically arranged in Taiwan, tending to keep both profits and tax revenues out of Palau'

The Taiwan market developed rapidly during the late 1990s, with visitor numbers rising beyond expectations. But there were drawbacks as well. "What was apparently at first a relatively high-end market shifted downward," one report noted. "Virtually all the visitors bought packaged tours . . . from tours to meals and entertainment—and most tours were arranged by wholesalers in Taiwan" (Levy 1999, 3ff). The same report decried the small share of the benefits that accrue to Palau. "Taiwanese-controlled tour operations tend to be highly vertically integrated, denying business opportunities to local businesses in many service areas. Tour packages are typically arranged in Taiwan, tending to keep both profits and tax revenues out of Palau" (Levy 1999, 3ff).

Table 2. Breakdown of Total by Country

Year	Total	Japan	Taiwan	Korea	China	US
1980	5,640	2,894				2,222
1981	5,057	2,650				1,676
1982	5,330	2,721				1,782
1983	6,388	3,026				1,989
1984	9,014	3,969				2,532
1985	13,371	6,968				3,214
1986	13,653	6,567				3,747
1987	16,695	6,924				4,205
1988	22,675	10,818				4,821
1989	26,005	11,633	648			6,060
1990	32,846	13,212	2,213			6,440
1991	32,700	14,529	1,953			6,411
1992	36,117	17,021	2,749			8,032
1993	40,497	18,554	4,171	888		7,861
1994	44,073	17,493	6,126	1,221		9,700
1995	53,229	21,052	11,163	1,823		9,846
1996	69,330	22,619	23,310	2,074	1,766	9,955
1997	73,719	20,507	31,246	1,782	1,447	10,481
1998	64,194	21,571	18,503	545	907	5,254
1999	55,493	22,087	10,936	539	868	5,587
2000	57,732	21,708	14,122	586	889	6,704
2001	54,111	22,395	12,476	350	867	5,375
2002	58,560	23,748	15,819	497	873	4,774
2003	68,296	21,401	27,857	312	250	4,291
2004	94,895	23,845	42,158	5,673	333	5,979
2005	86,124	26,281	34,101	2,169	336	5,532
2006	87,206	26,751	28,449	11,756	386	5,922
2007	93,031	29,198	29,005	14,342	464	5,956
2008	83,114	30,018	19,981	14,186	439	5,235
2009	83,795	26,688	16,278	13,009	534	5,193
2010	92,500	29,318	22,161	15,144	725	5,809
2011	118,055	37,800	37,632	15,681	1,699	5,890
2012	124,117	39,353	38,649	19,465	4,471	6,530
2013	114,000	31,695	23,853	15,321	7,897	6,067
2014	146,867	38,610	30,466	14,808	39,936	9,298
2015	167,966	31,878	14,013	12,238	86,850	8,582

Notes:
Visitors 1984 includes 1,200 entering for employment, mainly from the Philippines.
Visitors from US, 1998–2014: these figures are much lower than previous ones because PVA breaks out US mainland from US Guam. Moreover, the later figures do not reflect those coming for business or employment.

Sources:
Visitor breakdown by country, 1980–1989: www.nps.gov/wpro/piso/peleliu/Table A; data derived from Division of Cultural Affairs, Palau; and PVA figures.
Visitor breakdown by country, 1998–2004: palaugov.org/immigration-tourism-statistics.
Visitor breakdown by country, 2000–2015: PVA figures used here for calendar year.

There were other problems as well. When Palauans gauged the new tourists against the standards set by early Japanese visitors, the Taiwanese were found wanting. Japanese, like Americans, generally visited Palau to scuba dive, while most Taiwanese came to do general sightseeing. In fact, the Taiwanese were unaccustomed to swimming and diving, and the large groups of tourists who wandered the shallows in Palau soon came to be viewed as a threat to the environment; there were frequent reports of Taiwanese tourists trampling coral and toss bits of sea life into their tote bags. Culturally less restrained and orderly than the Japanese, tourists from Taiwan soon established a reputation for being noisy and unruly. Finally, for all their numbers, the benefit of Taiwanese tourism on the Palau economy was minimal, for the visitors were coming on package tours, large numbers at a time, and spending next to nothing in local stores and restaurants. This was not the high-end, low-impact tourism that Palau had in mind when it embraced the development of the tourism industry in the late 1970s.[8]

Nonetheless, the Taiwan market was clearly a major factor in the enormous growth of Palau's tourism between 1986 and 1997. The number of visitors grew from 13,000 to 73,000—more than a five-fold increase during those 12 years (Table 1). Furthermore, the Taiwan trade has remained generally undiminished up to the present. Over the years Taiwan has been right behind Japan in the number of visitors to Palau, with its share of the total visitors registering at about 20 to 25 percent.

SLUMP IN THE ASIAN MARKET: 1998–2003

Suddenly, the major financial crisis that hit Asia in 1997 hobbled Asian economies and drastically curtailed the spending power of the middle class. The effects were immediately felt in Palau, where visitor numbers dropped from a high of 73,000 in 1997 to 64,000 the following year, and to 55,000 the year after that. Within two years, Palau had lost 25 percent of its yearly visitors. The Japanese market was largely unaffected by the crisis—the Japanese visitor count remained steady throughout the slump—but Taiwan visitor numbers plummeted from 31,000 in 1997 to just one-third of that (10,900) two years later (Table 1).

The uneven impact of the Asian financial crisis on Palau tourism prompted serious reflection on the nature of the market.

> The Taiwan economy weathered the 1997–1998 economic crisis better than most countries in the region, but better vacation deals offered by other Asian nations apparently decreased the appeal of Palau. No such shift occurred with Japanese visitation, a reminder that while Palau has something special to offer scuba divers and visitors interested in the history and culture of the Pacific, it has nothing unique to offer general vacationers seeking little more than sun, water, and night life (Levy 1999, 3).

Even before Palau felt the effects of the Asian financial crisis, planners there—prompted by what they felt was a downturn in the quality of tourism in recent years—were trying to bring about a shift in the market. In 1996, Mary Ann Delemel, then director of the Palau Visitors Authority (PVA), began serious efforts to develop the European market, especially for diving enthusiasts in Germany and Italy. The PVA contacted travel agents throughout Europe, presented at trade shows, and later offered agents retainers to represent Palau. This was difficult work, Delemel admitted in an interview, but she succeeded in creating a modest European market at the end of it all. The visitor numbers from Europe do not really do justice to their economic impact, she added. Europeans, who usually come by way of Manila or Taipei, tend to spend a longer time in Palau—often as long as two or three weeks—since their paid vacation leave is more generous than in the United States or Asia.[9] The efforts to increase the European market did not seem to have immediate success. The number of European visitors hovered at only 1,500 a year through the late 1990s, but by 2013 it had increased to about 3,700 (PVA 2014).

Due to the slump, some major construction projects, including a couple of major-brand hotels, went uncompleted. One of the abandoned projects involved the revival and expansion of the old Continental Hotel in a remote section of northern Koror. The other was the construction of a hotel and high-end condominium complex near the port on Malakal. The steel skeleton that stood on the site for years was a reminder of the dashed hopes of tourism growth at the beginning of the millennium (BOH 2003, 9).[10]

Tourism in Palau showed a modest rebound during 2002 and 2003, with an average growth rate of more than 10 percent during those years. This is surprising in view of the long list of setbacks to worldwide tourism during the same years: the September 11 terrorist attacks on the United States, the SARS epidemic, the Iraq War, and the ongoing US-sponsored War on Terror. In reality, most of these setbacks seemed to affect the US and European markets more than the Asian markets. Even so, the drop in the number of US visitors to Palau lasted no longer than two years. Overall, the terrorism scare and the fear of flying that resulted from it seemed to have had a minor impact on business in Palau. This is in sharp contrast to Guam and Northern Mariana Islands, which recorded drops of 50 to 70 percent in Japanese tourist traffic in the two years following 9/11 (BOH 2003, 9–10).

> The terrorism scare and the fear of flying that resulted from it seemed to have had a minor impact on business in Palau

A brief update on Palau issued by the US Department of the Interior in 2004 offered an upbeat picture of the tourism potential there:

A major private project completed recently is the Papago International Resort near the airport area. Completed in late 2002, the resort has 100 rooms and other amenities, targeting mainly Taiwanese tourists. The capital for the project came from Taiwan, along with management, and labor is provided by China. Beside the well-known Palau Pacific Resort and Palasia Hotel Palau, Koror now has three major hotels with 100 or more rooms and world-class facilities and services. Putting all hotel and motel rooms together, Palau now has a total room count of just over 1,000. That count is still much smaller than CNMI's more than 4,000 and Guam's 8,000–9,000 rooms, but a big increase from a decade ago (Osman 2004).

BOOM YEARS

The year 2004 was a banner year for tourism in Palau, with the number of visitors reaching an unprecedented 94,000, an increase of 40 percent in a single year. The boom occurred just as Palau hosted two events headlining the island nation throughout different parts of the world.

In the early summer, the 9th Annual Pacific Arts Festival was held in Palau, drawing hundreds of visitors from the Pacific and further abroad. As successful as the event was, it appears to have had no lasting impact on tourism patterns in Palau. Then later that year, Palau was selected to be the site of *Survivor*, an American reality-TV series. Filming *Survivor: Palau* took place in Koror for 39 days with 20 competitors. The program was aired early the following year to US audiences (Sakuma 2007). Like the Pacific Arts Festival, the *Survivor* series had no perceptible effect on long-term tourism. It did, however, result in the opening of two restaurants that have remained popular up to the present: Drop Off and Kramer's, both built when the TV series was being filmed (Jennifer Gibbons interview).

The sudden upswing in tourism in 2004 was clearly the result of other factors. The number of visitors from Taiwan had surged that year to 42,000—the highest number ever recorded for that market. In addition, the Korean market opened the same year, bringing over 5,000 visitors to Palau. Together these two markets accounted for a spike of 20,000 visitors in a single year (Table 1).

Prior to 2004, the number of Korean visitors to Palau had been negligible. In the mid-1990s, just as the Taiwan market was beginning to take off, between 1,000 and 2,000 Koreans were visiting Palau each year, but the number soon fell to about 500. Then, in 2004, the number of visitors suddenly climbed to over 5,000. HanaTour, a tourist agency with offices throughout coastal northern Asia, was responsible for this (Minoru Ueki 2014). It was HanaTour that arranged for the first charter flights from Seoul to Palau via Asiana Airlines. The number of Korean visitors grew to 14,000 in 2007 and has stayed at that level to the present (Table 1). Today the Korean market represents a solid share of the visitor business in Palau.

The tourism upswing, largely from Taiwan and South Korea, was a much-needed boon for the Palau economy because of the loss of the garment industry and the decline of fishing. As described in a report for the US Department of the Interior, Palau's economy was seriously threatened at the time:

> Palau's two main exports were fish and manufactured garments. The value of Palau's garment industry reached $33.6 million in 2002. The closing of the country's remaining garment manufacturer in early 2003 ended this budding export industry and left the fishing industry as the only major contributor in Palau's exports. As a result of the declining fish and garment industries, the value of Palau's exports dropped from $20.3 million in 2002 to $8.4 million and $5.8 million in 2003 and 2004 respectively (Sakuma 2007, 9).

This cast the role of tourism in a different light. No longer would it be looked upon to supplement other productive sectors of the economy. Henceforth it would be seen as the mainstay of the economy.

Soon afterward, Babeldaob, the major land mass in the Palau group of islands, was finally opened up for tourism. The collapse of the Koror-Babeldaob bridge in 1996, almost 20 years after it was originally opened, had cut the easy link between the population center and Babeldaob for a time. In 2002 a Japanese construction company finally replaced the bridge. Within a year or two, construction was begun on the 53-mile circumferential road around Babeldaob that was to be funded by the United States under the Compact agreement. With the completion in 2007 of what was called the Compact Road, distant parts of Babeldaob became accessible to tourists for the first time. Just a year earlier, the capitol building for the national government, long situated in Koror, was moved to Melekeok, a small town midway up the eastern side of Babeldaob. The move had long been planned as a means of sharing national resources with other parts of the island group and stimulating development in more remote areas. A few years earlier, the airport terminal, located in the southern end of that island, was rebuilt—an improvement that "now makes Palau's airport terminal facility comparable to other small but modern and functional facilities of the region" (Osmond 2004).

With these developments, visitors had ready access to some of the most interesting cultural and scenic sites in Palau. They include Lake Ngardok in Melekeok, ancient stone carvings, pillars for the meeting house built by the gods, according to Palauan legend, Taki Waterfall Park in Ngardmau, the old sites that the Yapese people visited to quarry their famous stone money, Bat Cave, the traditional meeting house in Airai, and several mangrove channels. Tourist expansion into Babeldaob inevitably followed. By 2011, for instance, a regional business magazine was publicizing one of the new attractions: "On June 2, a three-course zip-line began soaring over the Taki Waterfall Park in the state of Ngardmau, complementing Palau's underwater lure and breathtaking lush landscape aptly branded as the 'Rainbow's End'" (Cagurangan and Peterson 2011). Some believe that the future of tourism in Palau lies in Babeldaob.

Meanwhile, the expansion of air service to Palau continued. This increased service, fueled by the visitor traffic from Taiwan, Korea, and Japan, was highlighted in a 2007 report. "The launch of Asian Spirit Airline's service made a total of five airline companies serving Palau," the report noted (Sakuma 2007, 1). In addition to Asian Spirit, Continental Airlines, EVA, Far Eastern Air Transport and Japan Airlines were flying into Palau—some with regular routes and others on a charter basis. By 2007 Palau had flights from Japan, Korea, Taiwan, the Philippines, Australia (via Darwin), the Federated States of Micronesia (through Yap), and the United States (via Guam).

Visitor accommodations in Palau grew accordingly. By 2007, Palau had an inventory of 1,253 rooms, an increase of 200 rooms from four years earlier. The hotel-development projects underway, the report added, would further increase the number of hotel rooms in the next two to five years (Sakuma 2007, 22). One of these was the Sea Passion Hotel, which was opened in 2009 and famed for its Asian ambience. This 68-room hotel soon captured a good share of tourists from Europe, South Korea, and Taiwan, and it enjoyed an occupancy rate of 80 percent during the first half of 2012 (Jennifer Gibbons interview).

Tourism in Palau, which had dipped slightly during the years 2004–2006, recovered in 2007 before taking another dip because of the US financial crisis in 2007. For the next two years (2008 and 2009) the number of yearly visitors dropped by 10,000 to about 83,000 a year. Then, in 2010, tourism took off again and surpassed the 100,000-visitors mark for the first time. It was the old story repeated yet again: Just as events seemed to conspire to level Palauan tourism, the industry would experience a mysterious rebound and visitor numbers would reach a new high.

Just as events seemed to conspire to level Palauan tourism, the industry would experience a mysterious rebound

THE CHINESE MARKET

In 2011, as the latest tourist boom was bringing Palau beyond the threshold of 100,000 visitors a year, a new market kicked in: mainland China. Since the mid-1990s, China had flirted with Palau as a tourist destination much as South Korea had, but yearly visitors from China could be counted in the hundreds rather than the thousands. The Republic of Palau, after all, had spurned the People's Republic of China to establish diplomatic ties with Taiwan in 1994. To make matters worse, Palau had agreed to take in six Uighurs, Islamic tribal people from China, who had been detained for years in the Guantanamo Bay detention camp. Yet, the demand for nearby vacation spots for mainland China's increasingly wealthy population overrode whatever indignation the country might have felt toward Palau for its past disloyalty.[11]

The number of Chinese visitors increased between 2011 and 2013 from 1,700 to about 7,900, and exploded to 39,000 the following year (Table 2). The 2015 figure of 86,500 was not too much short of the 100,000 figure predicted by one author (Blanc 2015). There are existing hotels able to handle the growing volume of tourists; one of them is the Palau Vacation Hotel, a large resort at the entrance to Malakal. Several others are already being planned for the future, as the influx of Chinese visitors continues to grow exponentially. The dramatic increase in Chinese tourism, moreover, has given rise to old concerns among Palauans about the future of the industry and its negative effects on the small island group.

The sudden Chinese tourism upsurge has been just the latest wave in the series of Asian booms experienced in Palau. The Japanese market, still foundational for Palau, first swept over the island in the late 1980s and has remained steady since then. The Taiwanese boom, which began in the early 1990s, was even more sudden and has shown much more fluctuation over the years. Korean tourism, which started in earnest in 2004, has been smaller but more reliable. Then, within the last four years, mainland China visitors first began coming to Palau, via Hong Kong, in appreciable numbers. Up to now, the waves have not subsided but built on one another to create a tourist industry that, with 166,000 visitors in 2015, is the envy of the Pacific.

Palau's achievement is all the more remarkable in view of the decline of tourism in other parts of the northern Pacific. In the Northern Marianas, visitors peaked in 1997 at 720,000, dropped by 200,000 the following year, and fell by another 200,000 during the next 10 years (Marianas Visitors Authority 2014). Guam's plunge has not been as severe, but only in the past two or three years has it started to approach its past high of 1.4 million visitors in 1997 (Guam Visitors Bureau 2014). Palau may not have the numbers that these places have, but the relatively steady pace of its tourism growth has been little short of miraculous.

IMPACT OF TOURISM ON PALAU'S ECONOMY

Palau's geography and physical isolation limit the range of activities that can profitably be undertaken to develop its economy. Like other Pacific nations before it, Palau looked to an industry that transformed what might have been competitive trade disadvantages into benefits. Tourism is one industry that can turn the tables for small island nations. Remoteness, small size, and underdevelopment (insofar as it offers visibility of the traditional culture) can be an advantage in attracting tourists. Tourism, of course, did not spring up full-blown at one magical moment in Palau, but over time became the major industry in a tiny nation that had few viable alternatives.

The dramatic increase in Chinese tourism has given rise to old concerns among Palauans about the future of the industry and its negative effects on the small island group

The contribution of tourism to any national economy is notoriously difficult to measure

The contribution of tourism to any national economy is notoriously difficult to measure. The calculation of the economic benefits comes from estimates of what the average tourist has spent on hotel accommodations, food and entertainment, local purchases, sightseeing, and other services. Since it is nearly impossible to track all but the most obvious purchases made by tourists (i.e., hotel accommodations and certain tourist activities), national planners usually devise a formula for estimating the money spent in a destination that is based on exit surveys of past visitors. The formula is arrived at by multiplying the average length of stay by the estimated daily expenditure of people by nationality. The resulting figure, multiplied by the number of visitors, can generate an approximate total of tourist expenditures in a country like Palau.

Although this total may represent a reasonably close estimate of the money spent in Palau, there is the further question of how much of this money truly enters the local economy. With prepackaged tours handled by foreign agents, hotels owned by outside investors, and foreign employees who are likely to remit a substantial part of their salary, the impact of tourist expenditures on the local economy is usually considerably less than the figure itself might suggest. On the other hand, money spent by visitors has other indirect effects on the island economy. It provides jobs in ancillary services—for store clerks and taxi drivers, among others—that increasing employment and fueling additional spending in what is sometimes called a multiplier effect. The next section examines some rough indicators of how tourism has benefitted the economy of Palau.

Employment and Wages

One indication of the impact of tourism on Palau's economy is the growth of employment. Between 1990 and 2013, as the number of visitors increased fourfold, employment in Palau doubled from 5,438 to 10,999.[12] The number of jobs directly ascribed to the tourism industry over the same period also doubled—from 856 to 1,713.[13] But since these figures record only those individuals working in hotels and food services, they do not capture the full impact of the tourist boom on employment in the ancillary services—in positions such as tour guides and boat drivers. Additional jobs were created by the construction of new hotels and tourist facilities.

Not all these jobs were taken by Palauans, of course. Filipinos and Chinese make up a good part of the labor force, but the number of expatriates in Palau dropped between 2000 and 2012 from 5,765 to 4,631 (EconMAP 2014, Table 1a). Unemployment was measured at a mere 4.1 percent of the work force in 2012, so it can be assumed that jobs are available for any Palauans who want them (EconMAP 2014, Table 1b). This ready employment is not to be found in most Pacific nations.

Tax and Revenue

The increase in local revenue, which supplements the Compact funds Palau receives from the United States, is in good part another effect of the growth of the tourism industry. In 1994, the
Palau government had collected $18.3 million in local revenues. One year later, after the number of visitors to Palau had jumped by 21 percent, tax revenues increased by 14 percent, from $18.3 million to $20.9 million (US DOI 1995).

By 2013, the nation was collecting $41.4 million in revenue, largely from gross-revenue business taxes, personal income tax, and general import tax. The airport departure tax and the

Table 3. National GDP and Tourism Earnings (in current dollars)

Year	Total GDP ($,000,000)	Tourism Earnings ($,000,000)	Tourism Earnings/GDP %
2000	150.1	47	31
2001	160.7	42	26
2002	164.2	43	26
2003	160.5	44	26
2004	175.7	53	28
2005	193.5	62	30
2006	194.5	62	30
2007	195.7	70	33
2008	199	75	36
2009	186.8	75	36
2010	184.3	76	39
2011	201.2	95	45
2012	215.8	95	50
2013	228.6	118	50
2014	250.6	135	54

Sources:
GDP 2000–2014: EconMAP 2015, Table 2a.
Tourism Earnings 2000–2013: EconMAP 2014, Table 8d.
2014 figures: EconMAP 2015: Table 5d.

Green Fee—a tax on visitors that would be used to protect and maintain marine areas—have also boosted total revenues (EconMAP 2014, Table 9a). Tax revenues raised locally in 2013 ($41.4 million) were nearly equal to the total grant money the Palau government receives ($42 million), an amount that includes the Compact funds that the United States provides each year (EconMAP 2014, Table 9a).

Contribution to National Economy

The tourist explosion that occurred in 2003–2004 offers one example of how tourism expansion in Palau can be correlated with growth of the overall economy. In that period, the number of visitors to Palau skyrocketed from 68,000 to 95,000 (Table 1), and Palau's Gross Domestic Product (GDP) grew from $157 million to $172.9 million—an upswing of nearly $16 million that represented a 10 percent increase (EconMAP 2014, Table 2a). Admittedly, major construction work on the Compact road was being carried out at the same time, but the breakdown of the sectors showing high growth suggest that much of the rise in GDP could be attributed to the surge in tourism. Between 2003 and 2004, food services and accommodation grew from $10 million to $15 million, while real estate expanded from $5 million to nearly $11 million (EconMAP 2014, Table 2f).

Table 3 offers a comparative look at the rise of the estimated income from tourism and the increase of the total economy, or GDP, over the years 2000–2014. During that period, the contribution of visitors (listed under exports as "travel") to the economy is shown to have grown from

$45 million to $134.8 million (EconMAP 2014, Table 8d; EconMAP 2015, 5d). Meanwhile, the overall economy of Palau expanded from $147 million to nearly $251 million—a growth of 70 percent in 14 years. Even when adjusted for inflation, per capita GDP in current dollars increased during these years from $7,900 to over $14,150 (EconMAP 2015, Table 2a).

In 2014, tourist expenditures ($135 million) accounted for a little over half of Palau's total GDP ($250.6 million) (Table 3). The value of tourism for Palau far overshadows any other industry; tourism is recognized as the main contributor to the Palau economy today and remains the hope of the future.

Nowhere in the Pacific has tourism alone been able to sustain the national economy. Yet, in most Pacific Island nations, as a recent report of the Pacific Islands Forum Secretariat points out, tourism "continues to be the major driver of economic growth and foreign exchange earnings" (PIFS 2013, 3). The report goes on to cite a study showing that the "total (direct, indirect, and induced) contribution of tourism to the Pacific Island economies in 2012 was 2.7 percent of total GDP."[14] But the estimate for percent of total GDP for the Pacific is rated much higher by some. According to the World Travel and Tourism Council, "Tourism is vital to the sustainable growth of Pacific island economies, contributing an estimated 10.7 percent of the region's Gross Domestic Product (GDP) in 2012" (PIFS 2013, 6).

Other Pacific Islands might entertain more visitors each year than Palau. Fiji, with a population of nearly a million, records well over 600,000 visitors, while Samoa, with 220,000 residents, receives about 125,000 visitors a year. Vanuatu, with a population about the size of Samoa's, hosts nearly as many visitors (PIFS 2013, 7). But no other Pacific Island nation—not even the Cook Islands with their comparable population size and number of visitor entries—can claim that tourism contributes as large a share to its total GDP as Palau can (Hezel 2012). Even the other major tourist destinations that are not self-governing—Guam and the Northern Marianas in the northern Pacific and French Polynesia in the south—cannot match Palau's degree of reliance on this single industry.

No other Pacific Island nation can claim that tourism contributes as large a share to its total GDP as Palau can

SOME KEYS TO SUCCESS

Many Pacific Islands offer good beaches and natural beauty, but Palau's stunning dive sites put the island nation in a class of its own and became the engine for its growth. Most of the early Japanese tourists were divers, after all, and a sizable percentage of its current visitors are, too. Palau, as one article explained, is "protected by a barrier reef; it has deep water walls all the way around it. It has a lot of cold water upwelling which brings nutrients into the upper levels of the water column" (Cagurangan and Peterson 2011). Its splendid diving and the access this offers to its marine life—which includes more than 1,300 species of fish and over 700 types of coral—has merited Palau's inclusion in *National Geographic Traveler*'s "50 Places of a Lifetime: The World's Greatest Destinations."[15] Diving to explore the marine life of the islands quickly became the primary tourist attraction of Palau.[16]

Palau's location close to mainland Asia offers it a competitive advantage over most other island destinations. It is within easy flying distance of many of the most important cities of East Asia, including those that have represented the major growth markets over the past 30 years of its tourism development.

From the very outset Palauans responded favorably to foreign-investment proposals. The president of Tokyu Corporation's initial interest in building a first-class hotel in Palau was prompted by his easy dealings with Palauans, many of whom still spoke Japanese. The flow of visitors from Japan that followed the opening of the hotel provided the base for the future growth of the tourist industry well before other Asian markets opened up to Palau. This early arrangement, one in which both parties came to know one another personally and committed themselves to working out a mutually acceptable understanding of how the business would work, might have served as an excellent model for future development. The model was seldom observed, however, as investors from other Asian countries rushed to Palau in the last 25 years.

Palau's lack of a regulatory framework has helped the nation grow, one prominent Palauan businessman remarked, contrary to conventional wisdom and the prescription of most international financial institutions. Minimal government interference, he explains, has opened the door for outside investors to work directly with local businessmen. The social system in Palau with its own strong controls—including the intense cultural competitiveness and the "our-eyes-are-on-you" social climate—is more than adequate to guard local interests, he believes (Kaleb Udui interview).

A touch of the distinctive local flavor is something tourists want when they vacation in a place, as one person experienced in the travel industry pointed out. The form this local flavor takes might be as simple as passing encounters with Palauan employees working as waiters, tour guides, or boat operators. Despite the large number of Asians employed in the tourist industry in Palau, there are still many local people who accompany visitors on their tours and serve as diving guides (Jennifer Gibbons interview).

As its tourism industry has grown, Palau has found it helpful to offer products for sale with a local stamp. The local beer, Red Rooster, is just one example. The airport gift shop and some of the stores also offer lotions, cosmetics, and liquor with a distinctive Palauan brand name. In addition, Palau's famous storyboards carved in wood in bas-relief are offered for sale nearly everywhere. The touch of the local may not create a new tourist market, but it can certainly help sustain and grow markets once they exist.

THE FUTURE

Currently there are at least three major hotels planned for construction, two of them funded by investors from mainland China. The first is a 600-room hotel in Malakal, the islet at the southern tip of Koror that has become a favored site for recent tourist development. The land for this hotel has already been leased from Koror State. The second is a 300- or 400-room hotel that is to be built in Airai at the foot of the Koror-Babeldaob Bridge. The local partners in both projects are sons of Roman Tmetuchl, the former owner of the Airai View Hotel. The third is an 80-room hotel to be named The Wild Orchid and located in Malakal. Shalum Etpison, the son of Ngirakl Etpison, one of the founders of the Palau Pacific Resort, is financing the project and using his own local construction company to build this entirely Palauan-owned hotel.

As the demand for new hotels increases, Asian investors can be expected to step forward with proposals for new buildings and the funding to bankroll the investments. The pattern established in recent years has been for a Palauan to partner with an outside investor in compliance with Palau's foreign-investment regulations. The local partner, who must provide the land and obtain approval for the venture, will have a major share of the business, at least on

The social system in Palau, with its own strong controls, is more than adequate to guard local interests, says a local businessman

paper. In fact, however, the ownership and business decisions are almost entirely handled by the outside investors. "Our biggest issue has been front businesses for the last 10 years," said Mandy Etpison, the wife of a leading Palauan businessman. Her quote in a business magazine continued, "On paper, they're Palauan, but they are being managed and operated by foreigners such as the Taiwanese and Koreans" (Cagurangan and Peterson 2011).

Expectations are that the China market will burgeon even further in the years to come, leading to the demand for still more hotels on the island. Businessmen are already complaining that the number of hotel rooms is barely able to provide for the increase in visitors over the past few years. Everyone in Palau foresees the ongoing expansion of tourism in their islands. This is a dubious blessing for many, who worry that the recent influx of Asians from Taiwan and mainland China will drive away the Japanese—long considered the mainstay of the industry in Palau.

Some Palauans are happy with the prospect of expanded tourism in Palau but are more concerned with building up the high-end market. Steps have already been taken to entice more Europeans, known to stay longer and spend more. Some are committed to growing the US tourist market as well. American tourists are mainly divers, said Delemel, the former head of the PVA. "As such they are not big spenders since they have already invested heavily in their scuba gear and they spend all their time in the water, not in local stores or bars" (Mary Ann Delemel interview). But there is a small subset of that group comprised of wreck-diving enthusiasts—perhaps only a fraction of all divers, but better off financially and committed to returning to the best sites year after year. At one time Palau had more World War II shipwrecks than Chuuk, one person noted, but many of these wrecks were salvaged for their scrap metal in the years after the war. Delemel added that many Palauans today have come to rue this as short-sightedness.

Not everyone in Palau rejoices at the prospect of expanding tourism in the years ahead. Ordinary citizens often join environmentalists in expressing their fear that the ever higher numbers will do irretrievable damage to the coral, the beaches, and the marine life—those distinctive assets that attract visitors to the island group in the first place. They are fearful that the growing influx of visitors, for all the economic blessings they might bring to Palau, might undermine and perhaps destroy the "natural" endowments, whether ecological or cultural. They articulate the questions that others may hesitate to ask: How much tourism is enough? At what point do the damages of tourism begin to outweigh its advantages? Sustainable tourism, according to the United Nations, requires maintaining a suitable balance between three dimensions: the environmental resources of the place, the socio-cultural heritage of the host community, and the viable long-term economic benefits of the industry (Panakera et al 2011, 242–243).

How many tourists does Palau need? How many can it accommodate without doing harm to the ecosystem? "Informal long-term estimates range from 200,000 to 300,000 at this stage of development," an economic review of Palau in 2000 stated (BOH 2000, 18). But this report, published 15 years ago, appeared 20 years after planners in Palau projected an ideal ceiling of 30,000 or 40,000 visitors a year (Warner et al 1979, 10). Will the estimate again be revised upward as Palau, always in need of foreign exchange, now approaches the lower limits of the figure offered in 2000?

How much tourism is enough? At what point do the damages of tourism begin to outweigh its advantages?

REFERENCES

Publications

Blanc, Sebastien. 2015. "Chinese Descend on Remote Palau as Wanderlust Deepens." *Business Insider*, March 15. www.businessinsider.com/afp-chinese-descend-on-remote-palau-as-wanderlust-deepens-2015-3.

Cagurangan, Mar-Vic, and Jessica Peterson. 2011. "Palau in Progress: Reaching a New Height." *Guam Business*. July–August.

EconMAP. *See* Economic Monitoring & Analysis Program.

Economic Monitoring & Analysis Program. 2014. *Republic of Palau: Fiscal Year 2013 Economic Review*. Produced for Graduate School USA, Pacific Islands Training Initiative. Honolulu.

www.pitiviti.org/news/wp-content/uploads/downloads/2014/09/RoP_EconReview_FY13_Final _Jun2014.pdf.

———. 2015. *Republic of Palau: Fiscal Year 2014 Statistical Appendices* (for *Republic of Palau: Fiscal Year 2014 Economic Review*). Produced for Graduate School USA, Pacific Islands Training Initiative. Honolulu.

www.pitiviti.org/news/wp-content/uploads/downloads/2015/03/RoP_EconStat_tabs_FY14.pdf.

Etpison, Mandy. 2009. *Celebrating Palau*. Koror, Palau.

Guam Visitors Bureau. 2014. "Visitor Arrivals for FY 2014 Breaks Records." News release, October 10. www.guamvisitorsbureau.com/news/news-releases/visitor-arrivals-for-fy-2014-breaks-records.

Hezel, Francis X. 1984. "A Brief Economic History of Micronesia" in *Past Achievements and Future Possibilities: A Conference on Economic Development in Micronesia, Pohnpei, May 22–25*. Micronesian Seminar. www.micsem.org/pubs/articles/economic/frames/ecohistfr.htm.

———. 1995. *Strangers in Their Own Land: A Century of Colonial Rule in the Caroline and Marshall Islands*. Pacific Islands Monograph Series, no. 13. Honolulu: University of Hawai'i Press.

———. 2012. *Pacific Island Nations: How Viable Are Their Economies?* Pacific Islands Policy, no. 7. Honolulu: East-West Center. www.eastwestcenter.org/publications/pacific-island-nations-how-viable-are-their-economies.

Hezel, Francis X., and Michael J. Levin. 1990. "Micronesian Emigration: The Brain Drain in Palau, Marshalls and the Federated States." In *Migration and Development in the South Pacific*, ed. John Connell, 42–60. Canberra: Australian National University.

Levy, Karen. 1999. "Palau's Taiwanese Tourism Industry: Assessment of Issues and Suggestions for the Future." Palau Conservation Society Report 99–04. February.

Marianas Visitors Authority. 2014. Visitor Arrival Statistics, 1978–2013. Saipan, Commonwealth of the Northern Mariana Islands. Digital files.

Osman, Wali. 2000. *Republic of Palau: Economic Report*. Honolulu: Bank of Hawai'i and East-West Center.

———. 2003. *Republic of Palau: Economic Report*. Honolulu: Bank of Hawai'i and East-West Center. www.eastwestcenter.org/publications/republic-palau-economic-report.

———. 2004. "An Update on the Economy of Palau." US Department of the Interior, Office of Insular Affairs Economic Reports and Updates.

www.doi.gov/oia/reports/upload/A-Brief-Update-on-Palau.pdf.

Pacific Islands Forum Secretariat. 2013. "Tourism as a Pillar of Economic Growth." Presented at Session 2 of Forum Economic Ministers Meeting. Nuku'alofa, Tonga, July 3–5.

Palau Visitors Authority. 1980–2014. Statistics on Visitors to Palau. Digital files in PVA archives.

Panakera, Charlie et al. 2011. "Considerations for Sustainable Tourism Development in Developing Countries: Perspectives from the South Pacific." *Tourismos: An International Multidisciplinary Journal of Tourism*. Vol. 6:2. Autumn, 241–262.

PIFS. *See* Pacific Islands Forum Secretariat.

PVA. *See* Palau Visitors Authority.

Sakuma, Sharon. 2007. *Republic of Palau Business Opportunities Report*, updated by Pearl Ueranant. Prepared for the US Department of Interior, Office of Insular Affairs.

US Department of Interior. 1995. "Report on Palau." Chapter 6 in *Report of the State of the Islands*. Office of Insular Affairs. Washington, DC: Government Printing Office.

US Department of State. 2013. "2013 Investment Climate Statement for Palau." Washington, DC. www.state.gov//e/eb/rls/othr/ics/2013/204586.htm.

US DOI. *See* US Department of the Interior.

US DOS. *See* US Department of State.

Warner, Don, James A. Marsh, and Bruce G. Karolle. 1979. "The Potential of Tourism and Resort Development in Palau: A Socio-Economic-Ecological Impact Study." Study submitted to Pacific Islands Development Corporation. Mangilao, Guam: University of Guam. June.

Zolli, Andrew, and Ann Marie Healy. 2012. "A Tropical Tale of Tourists, Networks, and A New Kind Of Leadership." Fast Company. July 11. www.fastcompany.com/1842367/tropical-tale-tourists-networks-and-new-kind-leadership.

Interviews

Bernie Besebes	Operations Manager, Palau Visitors Authority
Mary Ann Delemel	Executive Director, Council of Chiefs
Kel Etpison	Son of the owner of Neco Enterprises

Shallum Etpison	Owner of Neco Enterprises
Jennifer Gibbons	Executive director, Palau Chamber of Commerce
Dermot Keane	Managing director, Sam's Tours
Glenn McKinley	Economist and consultant
Faustina Rehuher-Marugg	President, Palau Resource Institute
Kadoi Ruluked	Marketing and research manager, Palau Visitors Authority
Kaleb Udui, Jr.	Owner, Re/Max Gold Fern Realty, Palau
Minoru Ueki	Former Palau ambassador to Japan

NOTES

[1] Continental soon opened a route of its own between Palau and Manila. Shortly afterwards, the competition forced Air Nauru to suspend its own activities.

[2] One of the original partners, Benjamin Orrukum, sold out to the other two when he became ill; interview with Shallum Etpison.

[3] The resort has added another 60 rooms since 1985, runs at about 90 percent occupancy, and brings in $21 million a year in room rental alone; interview with Shallum Etpison.

[4] Minoru Ueki, in an interview, pointed out that in more recent years the Japanese market has tilted toward sightseers rather than scuba divers.

[5] The hotel was renovated afterwards and reopened. It functions up to the present, but has never been very popular with Japanese; most of its guests these days are Chinese.

[6] Palau again hosted the Festival ten years later, in 2004.

[7] Far-Eastern Air Transport has since failed, but China Airlines along with Asiana has continued to maintain service up to the present with five flights a week.

[8] The Palau Conservation Society wrote a full report on the Taiwanese tourist threat to the environment, but the report covers other problems with this market as well; see Levy 1999.

[9] The cultivation of the European market was a theme in many of the interviews done for this study, especially interviews with Mary Ann Delemel and Kadoi Ruluked.

[10] The half-built hotel, abandoned during the slump, was in fact completed in 2010 and named the Sea Passion Hotel; interview with Jennifer Gibbons, September 18, 2014.

[11] Despite the rapid growth in the number of Chinese tourists, there are still serious restrictions imposed by the Chinese government. Travel agencies in mainland China could get their license revoked by booking tours to Palau, and Chinese travelers still cannot obtain travel insurance for a trip to Palau (Cagurangan and Peterson 2011).

[12] Labor force statistics for 1990, along with other data from earlier years, were gathered from the Palau Government by Glenn McKinley. Figures for 2013 are found in EconMAP 2014, Table 3a.

[13] The figures for tourist industry employment in 1991 are again from Glenn McKinley, while the 2013 data come from EconMAP 2014, Table 3d.

[14] 2012 Economic Impact report by the World Travel and Tourism Council, cited by PIFS 2013, 3.

[15] Palau was nominated as one of the top 50 destinations in *National Geographic Traveler*, October 1999; cited in Cagurangan and Peterson 2011.

[16] A survey of visitors in 1995 showed that close to 60 percent of all visitors claimed that their main reason for visiting Palau was scuba diving (US DOI 1995). The figure appears to be unchanged since then.

Marianas Tourism

INTRODUCTION

Saipan, the capital of the Commonwealth of the Northern Mariana Islands (CNMI), is an island that has undergone one disaster after another but after each has been somehow reborn. Along with most of the Northern Mariana Islands, Saipan had its entire population relocated on Guam soon after the Spanish took possession of the island group three and a half centuries ago. It was only two centuries later, in the late 1800s, that the island was resettled—this time by seafaring Caroline Islanders along with the aboriginal Chamorro population. The island remained a backwater for some years until the 1920s and 1930s when it became a major Japanese colony with thousands of Japanese and Okinawan settlers. After World War II, it reverted to a sleepy outpost until the 1960s when it experienced a sudden burst of growth after it became the capital of the Trust Territory of the Pacific. Soon afterward, Saipan turned into a major tourist destination, and then plummeted as quickly as it had expanded. But the island has long grown accustomed to such ups and downs.

Saipan still has a bountiful tourist industry despite a sudden drop after 1997 and, within 14 years, saw its visitor numbers in 2011 decline to fewer than half of what they had been at their peak. Garapan, the commercial center and main tourist magnet on the island, has many of the largest hotels. Three of these, with a total of more than 800 rooms, are on the beach: the Hyatt Regency and Fiesta Resort and Spa, side by side next to the popular Micronesian Beach, and the Hafadai Beach Hotel down the road a half mile, situated within easy walking distance of the numerous shops and restaurants that cater to Asian tourists. Nearby are the spacious Duty Free Shop, Hard Rock Cafe, Winchell's Donut House, and dozens of sushi and sake places.

Tourists view a gun left behind after World War II at a former command post in Saipan, Northern Marianas. *Photograph by Norden Cheatham.*

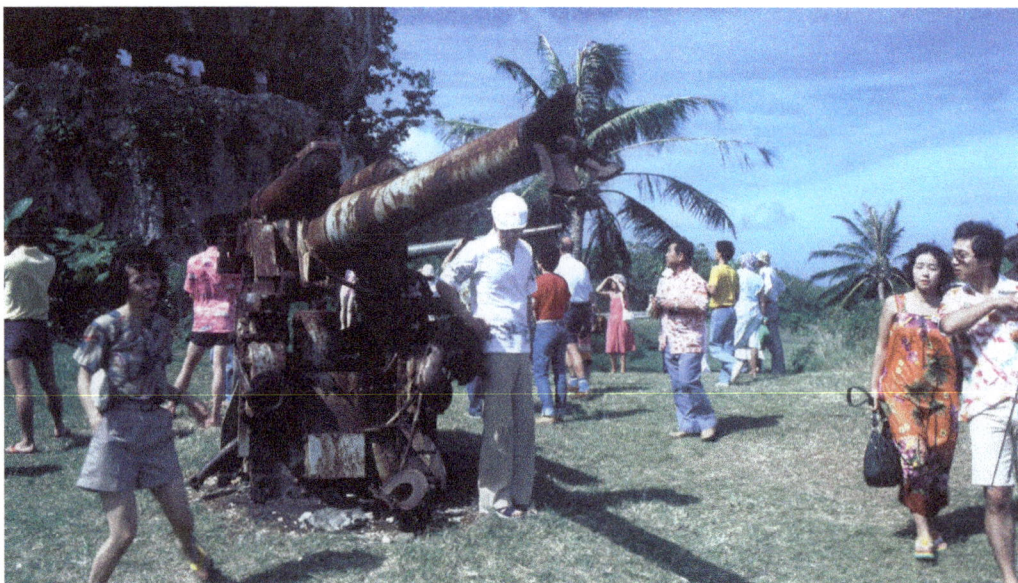

For Japanese tourists, who once comprised two-thirds of the total visitors, there are many historical features of interest. Japan governed the Marianas for 30 years, but lost them to American forces in 1944 as the war was nearing an end. Garapan itself, overflowing with Japanese and Okinawans during the end of the Japanese era, holds special significance for those who know and care about the history of the place. The monument to the Sugar King—a statue of Haruji Matsue, the founder of the sugar industry on Saipan—and an old railroad engine are reminders of the days when sugar was grown in nearly every bit of arable land.[1] Then there are the World War II sites, most of them in the northern part of Saipan: the caves in which Japanese and local islanders found refuge during the bombardment prior to the invasion, the artillery guns and old Japanese airfield, the Last Command Post where the Japanese commandant committed suicide, and the towering bluffs from which civilians and military jumped to their death just before the island was finally taken by American troops.

As visitors drive south along Beach Road, lined with beautiful flame trees that blossom in a brilliant red during late spring, they come to the village of Chalan Kanoa. It was the main settlement throughout the early post-war years until, with the burst of tourism in the 1980s, business and so much else shifted north again to Garapan. Chalan Kanoa today wears a ghostly pall, its closed shops a reminder of better days when the garment industry flourished and supported the large Chinese and Filipino migrant population brought in to work in the clothing factories.

There are the usual tourist attractions to be found in any semitropical getaway—beaches, sunset cruises, and golf courses (cheap by Japanese and Korean standards)—but Saipan seems different from the rest. Its history hangs heavy over the island; perhaps this is a large part of its appeal.

Saipan's history hangs heavy over the island; perhaps this is a large part of its appeal

BACKGROUND

Saipan, with a land mass of 47 square miles, is but one of 14 major islands in the Northern Mariana Islands, although the majority of these are uninhabited. Only Rota and Tinian, Saipan's nearest neighbors to the south, have a significant resident population. The current population of the entire island group is 52,300, down from nearly 70,000 a decade and a half ago. All but 4,000 live on Saipan, the capital and the commercial center of the Commonwealth (CIA 2015).

The twentieth-century colonial history of the Northern Marianas is essentially the same as that of Palau and Chuuk. US forces invaded Saipan, as they did Palau, and retook the islands, using the airstrip on Tinian to launch the B-29s that dropped atomic bombs on Hiroshima and Nagasaki in August 1945. At the end of the World War II, the United States administered the islands as a Strategic Trust Territory for the next 30 years.

Like Palau and Chuuk, the Northern Marianas was a district of the Trust Territory of the Pacific Islands under US administration. Almost immediately, however, the Northern Marianas, with the single exception of Rota, was cordoned off from the rest of the Trust Territory and turned over to US Naval administration. Saipan became the site of a CIA-run training facility to prepare Chinese nationalists for an assault on the Communist mainland. Only in 1962 were the Northern Marianas reunited under the administration of the US Department of the Interior.

Almost immediately afterward, Saipan was named the capital of the Trust Territory, and the expanding government workforce was moved into the housing abandoned by the CIA. Situated on the highest peak on the island, the locale soon was given the name Capitol Hill. With the pro-development reforms during the administration of US President John F. Kennedy, the island experienced rapid expansion. Its population, which had numbered barely 4,000 at the end of the war and had expanded to about 7,000 in 1960, grew within a few years to over 12,000, including the employees of the Trust Territory Government, the islands' major employer (Osman 2003, 4). From a sleepy backwater, Saipan suddenly took on the sheen of a government center, with new businesses opening, and bars and stores springing up everywhere. For the next several years, Saipan became the metropole of the Trust Territory, with travelers coming from all the island groups to do business there. Manpower was being moved in, money was being spent on infrastructure and government operations, and business flourished as it had not since the height of the Japanese occupation. The island was in a rapid growth cycle even before tourism began to take off.

The Northern Marianas sent an elected delegation to the newly formed Congress of Micronesia in 1966, but from the start, they found themselves distant relatives at best to the representatives from the rest of Micronesia. While the other districts were weighing the advantages of independence against other political options, the Northern Marianas lost no time in making plain its desire to affiliate permanently with the United States. In 1972, the United States agreed to hold separate political status talks with the Northern Marianas, which by that time had become the wealthy member of the Micronesian family. Negotiations, which began in 1972, led to the adoption of a commonwealth in political union with the United States that was approved in 1975 and came into force the following year. With this, the Northern Marianas severed its ties with the rest of the Trust Territory and became the first of the six districts to finalize its political status.[2]

SEEDS OF TOURISM (1968–1975)

The seeds of tourism in Saipan were sown while the Northern Marianas was still part of the Trust Territory. With Micronesia weighing its future political options and taking its first hesitant steps to build an economy, Continental Airlines entered the scene and offered the hope of a serious tourist industry. Prior to this, virtually all travel within Micronesia was for business purposes. "Before 1968 travelers stayed at small government-operated hotels, most of them averaging ten rooms in size, which were more like boarding houses," wrote Mike Ashman, the Trust Territory head of tourism. "Now there are nearly 900 rooms in more than three dozen hotels ranging in size from tiny modified private homes to a 200-room resort," he boasted just six years later (Ashman 1974, 135).

From the start, expansion of the visitor industry in Saipan outpaced every other island in Micronesia. In 1968, Saipan received about 8,000 out of 13,000 total visitors to the Trust Territory for that year. The next year, the visitor tally for Saipan doubled to 16,200 (TT 1969). Saipan was the main beneficiary of the expanded air service because of its location—close to Guam (only 130 miles to the south) and Japan (within three hours flying time)—but its improved facilities after the buildup of the island during the 1960s also contributed. Still, by the end of 1969, there were only 238 hotel rooms in all of Micronesia suitable for international visitors, according to a report on Trust Territory tourism. Of the hotel rooms, the Northern Marianas had 107, or nearly half, most of them in Saipan. Hafa Adai Hotel and the Saipan Hotel, typical of the hotels in operation at that time, were modest facilities offering a total of

From the start, expansion of the visitor industry in Saipan outpaced every other island in Micronesia

30 rooms between them (TT 1970, 6). The Hafa Adai consisted of no more than 10 plywood bungalows, each a little larger than a shipping container (Stewart 2012).

The great leap forward for Saipan was the opening of the Royal Taga Hotel, an imposing edifice built on the beach that offered 60 rooms and provided such conveniences as a beauty shop, a barber shop, and an outdoor swimming pool with a cocktail lounge at the poolside. It was the first large hotel built in Saipan and a sign of what was to come.[3]

The growth in the number of visitors during the early 1970s, while not startling, was steady. Between 1971 and 1973, the number of visitors to the Northern Marianas—that is, to Saipan, for all practical purposes—increased from 19,000 to 35,000.[4] The growth continued at about the same rate for the next two years, so that by 1975, the Northern Marianas reached just short of 50,000 visitors. Saipan was the destination of two-thirds of all the visitors to the Trust Territory during those years (US 1975). By then, the Royal Taga was no longer the only major hotel on the island. Continental Airlines had built a massive hotel on the beach in Garapan in 1973, and the Intercontinental Hotel was soon erected alongside it.[5] A few large hotels were built well south of Garapan in the Susupe and Chalan Kanoa area, and the total number of hotel rooms approached 500. By the time the Northern Marianas separated from the Trust Territory and was on the verge of entering into a formal commonwealth agreement with the United States, its tourist industry was growing by more than 20 percent annually and was well on its way to becoming a key sector of the economy (Table 1).

Meanwhile, the rest of the Trust Territory, fearful that a major tourist industry would do irreparable damage to the culture and replicate Waikiki throughout the islands, debated the role of tourism in Micronesia. Controls on tourism were urged everywhere in the Trust Territory, just as warnings were issued against making the economy entirely dependent on tourism. A territory-wide conference held in Yap in 1972 produced agreement on two main points: "1) Tourism can bring economic benefits and is probably the quickest way to generate income for an area, 2) but tourism must be seen as only one source of income, and agriculture and marine resources should also be developed" (*Honolulu Advertiser* 1972).

Yet, the Marianas was becoming heavily invested in tourism even at that early date, perhaps because leaders recognized the futility of other industrial paths. Just a month before the Yap conference, Francisco Diaz, chairman of the Marianas Tourist Commission and member of the district legislature, put the matter plainly: "Tourism is the only hope we have for staying alive economically in this increasingly expensive world." He added, "All we have going for us are warm, friendly people, a wonderful semitropical climate and great natural beauty" (*Honolulu Advertiser* 1971b).

LAYING THE FOUNDATION (1975–1979)

The three years following the decision by the Northern Marianas to adopt commonwealth status in 1975 and the full implementation of the new government in 1978 was a period dedicated to crafting its new political system. Tourism statistics are difficult to find for those interim years, but the political leaders of the Northern Marianas were well aware that tourism would be a large part of its future and negotiated accordingly on behalf of provisions that might have a bearing on its development. Exemption from restrictions on immigration and visa requirements was one major issue; a second issue was exemption from different types of US taxes and tariffs.

As Saipan boomed, the rest of the Trust Territory worried about cultural damage and replicating Waikiki in the islands

Table 1. Total CNMI Visitors and Hotel Rooms

Year	Visitors	Hotel Rooms	Year	Visitors	Hotel Rooms
1967			1992	488,330	2,852
1968	c8,000		1993	536,263	3,199
1969	16,200	86	1994	583,557	3,346
1970		107	1995	654,375	3,458
1971	19,316		1996	721,935	3,583
1972	25,143		1997	726,690	3,881
1973	35,819		1998	526,298	4,642
1974	44,438		1999	491,602	4,556
1975	49,130		2000	526,111	4,551
1976			2001	497,696	4,521
1977			2002	424,932	4,317
1978	86,708	765	2003	458,444	
1979	100,357	755	2004	531,584	
1980	110,755	740	2005	529,557	
1981	114,912	814	2006	443,812	
1982	111,173	767	2007	395,360	4,330
1983	124,024	816	2008	396,497	
1984	131,823	765	2009	375,808	
1985	142,284	975	2010	368,186	
1986	157,207	1,152	2011	338,106	3,511
1987	186,203	1,421	2012	389,475	
1988	233,291	1,824	2013	433,925	
1989	302,179	2,268	2014	443,963	
1990	417,146	2,651	2015	479,679	
1991	424,459	2,592			

Sources:
Visitors 1968–1969: TT Tourism Status Report 1969.
Visitors 1971–1975: US State Dept, TT Annual Reports.
Visitors 1978–2015: MVA, Visitor Arrival Statistics.
Hotels 1969: TT Tourism Status Report 1969.
Hotels 1970: TT "Travel Information" 1970.
Hotels 1978–2002: BOH 2003: 11.
Hotels 2007, 2011: MVA 2012.

Even before the finalization of its commonwealth status, business leaders in the Northern Marianas had successfully lobbied to have the prohibition of foreign investment removed.[6]

Growth in tourism continued during the late 1970s, with the number of visitors doubling in just four years—from 50,000 in 1975 to 100,000 in 1979 (Table 1). In the Northern Marianas as in Guam, Japanese visitors drove tourism expansion. In 1971, the *Honolulu Advertiser* noted the rapid increase of Japanese visitors to Guam—"from 4,000 in 1967 to an estimated 50,000 in 1970"—and projected nearly a fivefold increase by 1975 (*Honolulu Advertiser* 1971a). The

Table 2. Visitors to Northern Marianas by Nation

Year	Total	Japan	United States	Korea	China	Russia
1967						
1968	c8,000					
1969	16,200					
1970						
1971	19,316					
1972	25,143					
1973	35,819					
1974	44,438					
1975	49,130					
1976						
1977						
1978	86,708	58,812	24,901			
1979	100,357	74,094	23,026			
1980	110,755	84,448	21,519			
1981	114,912	91,801	19,544			
1982	111,173	89,806	17,992			
1983	124,024	101,521	18,259	1,002		
1984	131,823	104,156	22,511	938		
1985	142,284	108,455	26,258	1,608		
1986	157,207	122,618	26,877	1,854		
1987	186,203	145,008	34,045	2,560		
1988	233,291	182,793	41,488	3,695		
1989	302,179	227,529	54,813	10,451		
1990	417,146	314,144	69,070	17,034		
1991	424,459	308,395	72,916	20,184		
1992	488,330	345,971	79,142	31,165		
1993	536,263	374,727	78,132	52,963		
1994	583,557	388,170	79,012	91,155		
1995	654,375	409,855	95,516	124,007		
1996	721,935	437,880	90,049	168,517		
1997	726,690	450,190	77,078	169,822	2,487	
1998	526,298	396,228	64,100	39,281	3,042	
1999	491,602	372,101	32,465	45,691	2,241	
2000	526,111	381,518	34,038	67,979	1,337	
2001	497,696	373,517	20,285	62,956	2,094	
2002	424,932	293,932	16,007	77,665	7,008	
2003	458,444	318,225	15,884	79,831	13,351	
2004	531,584	384,845	14,491	69,480	29,238	
2005	529,557	376,263	17,013	65,049	32,441	

Table 2 continued

Year	Total	Japan	United States	Korea	China	Russia
2006	443,812	280,292	11,497	80,764	36,978	1,571
2007	395,360	215,196	8,546	98,403	41,024	3,043
2008	396,497	202,041	12,432	116,710	31,095	6,178
2009	375,808	210,567	10,949	92,995	27,859	6,801
2010	368,186	182,820	9,713	108,079	40,712	4,329
2011	338,106	148,634	8,928	106,483	46,451	5,092
2012	389,475	150,292	8,398	127,197	78,928	5,611
2013	433,925	148,423	7,438	135,458	112,570	11,002
2014	443,963	114,366	8,567	131,123	157,611	13,856
2015	479,679	88,582	8,079	181,952	181,465	2,769

Sources:
Visitors 1968–1969: TT Tourism Status Report 1969.
Visitors 1971–1975: US State Dept, TT Annual Reports.
Visitors 1978–2015: MVA, Visitor Arrival Statistics.

flow of Japanese tourists into Saipan, which began with the introduction of Air Micronesia into the area in 1968, was growing apace. In 1979, Japanese visitors numbered 74,000 and constituted three-quarters of the total market (Table 2). Virtually all the remaining visitors came from the United States, including the territory of Guam. While the US market remained the same during the next few years, the number of Japanese visitors increased. For the immediate future at least, the visitor industry in the Northern Marianas was tied to Japanese expansion.

Japan's people, flush with the nation's new prosperity, were looking for new vacation spots. In the Northern Marianas, Japanese tourists found a destination in which they felt comfortable. Saipan provided a warm vacation spot for swimming and enjoying the beach. But they also were visiting a place with strong historical ties to their own country: the prominence of the sugar industry before the war, the large Japanese settlement in Garapan with traces still visible, and the reminders everywhere of the sacrifices made during the final battle for Saipan.

For the first few years, tourist accommodations were provided by a number of smaller hotels that were locally owned. In a talk given at a Pacific-wide tourism conference in 1974, Mike Ashman could boast that "of Micronesia's 40 hotels today, 34 are wholly owned by Micronesians." He went on to note that "so far the marketing carried out . . . has been by private businesses: the airlines, hotels, shipping lines, travel agents and wholesalers, and others in the private sector" (Ashman 1974, 135). When Continental Airlines arrived with a fleet of planes and grand plans to develop Asian routes, it had the effect of mobilizing local resources to develop tourism. Most of the initial marketing as well as the early investment in hotels and other facilities came from island businessmen, sometimes in partnership with the airlines. To help coordinate these efforts, the Northern Marianas established its own visitors bureau in 1976.[7]

All this may have been adequate in the early years of tourism, but the growth of visitor numbers soon outpaced the ability of local businessmen to furnish the new hotels needed. Addi-

Japan's people, flush with the nation's new prosperity, were looking for new vacation spots

tional hotels and visitor facilities would have to be built to accommodate the growing flow of visitors.

Fortunately, the Northern Marianas offered liberal investment opportunities, thanks to the provisions of its recently signed Covenant with the United States. By virtue of that document the commonwealth offered many tax advantages for Asian and American investors. As one author summarized it,

> Business corporations in the Northern Marianas are generally treated as foreign for US tax purposes and do not pay federal tax to the US treasury on income earned in the CNMI. (By contrast, such corporations are generally subject to IRS tax on any income earned in other US jurisdictions.) The CNMI has no real estate or sales taxes. These incentives helped to entice substantial foreign investment... which fueled the islands' private sector development (Quimby 2013, 468).

Japanese investors, who could not fail to see the tourist potential of Saipan, had cash in hand ready to take advantage of these favorable terms of investment.

RAPID EXPANSION (1985–1997)

The early 1980s were a time of modest growth compared to what the Northern Marianas had already witnessed and even more so by comparison with what was to come (Table 1). But from 1985 to 1996, the Commonwealth experienced unprecedented growth in the number of visitors, generally at a double-digit annual percentage. Between 1987 and 1990, a period that saw visitor figures explode from 186,000 to 417,000, the yearly growth rate vaulted to 30 percent. The single year of greatest growth was 1989–1990, when the visitor total jumped from 302,000 to 417,000 (Table 1).

Tourism growth during the late 1980s far exceeded the most optimistic expectations of those promoting the industry. In 1986, the Marianas Visitors Bureau anticipated that if the growth rate continued, the number of tourists would hit 250,000 by 1990 (Phillips 1986), but actual tourist numbers skyrocketed to 417,000.

Japanese visitors in search of sun and sand fueled this growth, with Palau just opening up as another favored tourist spot. Between 1985 and 1990, the yearly visitor total in the Northern Marianas expanded from 108,000 to 314,000. Japanese still made up 75 percent of the total visitors, although a Korean market began to develop during the mid-1980s. From a few thousand during the late 1980s, it grew into a substantial market of 169,000 by 1997 (Table 2).

With the influx of Japanese visitors came investments from Japan. The country, still enjoying its newfound prosperity, was on the lookout for new overseas projects to fund.[8] "In the late 1980's and early 1990's, Japanese investors came to the islands and built resort hotels, golf courses and other tourist attractions," a Marianas Visitors Authority (MVA) report recalled. "Japanese organizations and individuals erected numerous memorials to people who lost their lives in the islands during World War II" (MVA 2012, 12). Another writer remembered it as "a time when Japanese bone collectors returned to the islands to collect the bones of Japanese soldiers for cremation and honorable burial at Yasukuni Shrine in Tokyo" (Stewart 2011).

Development of tourism on Saipan in the mid-1980s reached a new level. Hotel renovation and construction produced new facilities nearly each month, an article in the August 1986 issue of *Guam Business News* pointed out. Yet, the tourist boom had not entirely bypassed the older establishments. "Small hotels, such as the 14-room Pacific Gardenia Hotel in Chalan Kanoa, have found a niche in Saipan's tourist industry. Those smaller inns supply a total of 150 rooms" (Phillips 1986). By 1990 there were eight such hotels operating on Saipan, nearly all of them locally owned.

A few of those smaller hotels had been converted, often piecemeal through Japanese investors, into something far grander. The most impressive example was the Hafadai Beach Hotel, which could claim to be Saipan's largest hotel in 1985 after adding a 66-room wing the year before and soon afterwards dedicating its new stepladder-design tower. The expanded Hafadai with its 280 rooms had begun as no more than a 14-room beach property, one of the very first hotels on the island (Phillips 1986). The Surf Hotel, originally built with 37 rooms, had plans to add 71 rooms in 1986 and then another 90 rooms soon afterward (MVA 2012, 14).

Much of the new hotel construction, Phillips's article pointed out, took place outside the tourist area of Garapan in other parts of the island. In the village of Susupe, the 10-story Diamond Hotel had 326 rooms. Hotel Nikko, nearly as large, was being built in San Roque to the north and was completed in early 1988. Not to be outdone, the Hyatt Regency added 75 more rooms to its existing 183. Pacific Island Club, located in the southern part of the island, opened its 220-room facility in 1989 (Phillips 1986).

In all, the number of hotel rooms on Saipan topped 1,000 during the summer of 1986 (Table 1). The Northern Marianas Visitors Bureau boldly predicted that the number would double two years later by the end of 1988 (Phillips 1986). The bureau wasn't far off in its prediction: Saipan's hotel rooms reached 2,000 by 1989, even as the unprecedented growth continued.

By 1986, as the wave of Japanese tourists grew, Air Micronesia added flights to its Tokyo route, which it had inaugurated just a few years earlier, and flights from Osaka and Fukuoka. Japan Airlines (JAL) was in operation by the late 1980s. To better handle the greater tourist flow and the increased airline traffic, a new airport terminal was opened on Saipan in May 1989.[9]

Even if the Marianas were a world apart from Japan culturally and environmentally, the flying time there was only three hours

The reasons for this enormous tourist boom in the Northern Marianas are not hard to identify. The early burst of visitors through the 1980s came from Japan, although both the US and Korean markets developed substantially by the end of that decade. Japan was wealthy enough by that time that a great number of its citizens could afford to travel. Saipan was a natural choice of destination for those planning a vacation abroad since it offered them a complete change of venue, but still maintained vestiges of the old bonds that had once tied Japan to the islands. Moreover, even if the Marianas may have been a world apart from Japan culturally and environmentally, the flying time there was only a matter of three hours and the airline link was already in operation, thanks to Continental Airlines.

To provide further impetus to the tide of tourism, the Japanese government sponsored its "Ten Million Plan," the objective of which was to double the number of overseas travelers during the five-year period ending in 1991 (MVA 2006, 52). Japanese, who were "flush with wealth and looking for ways to invest in US property" anyway, easily provided the financial backing needed to build new hotels to house the growing number of visitors (MVA 2006, 12). During the last half of the 1980s alone, Japanese investors "poured close to a billion dollars in the Northern Marianas to develop the islands" (MVA 2006, 12). This was a time of great hotel construction, with hopes pinned heavily on the growing Japanese market. Indeed, the Japanese market peaked just short of half a million visitors a year in 1997 (Table 2).

Meanwhile, Saipan was attracting the attention of another Asian nation. By 1990, "the Korean visitor market also began to boom and Saipan saw the construction of small hotels, land tour operators, and support businesses catering to Koreans" (MVA 2006, 12). As in the case of Japan, Koreans themselves provided much of the investment for their own market. "Many Korean families moved to the island to develop businesses," the MVA report noted. The Korean market grew quickly and peaked in 1997 at 169,000 visitors, some 35 percent of the total visitors to the Northern Marianas (MVA 2006, 12).

While tourism was expanding rapidly, Saipan experienced the sudden emergence of a second economic windfall: the garment industry. The garment factories that began to pop up around the island beginning in the late 1980s employed seamstresses to do finishing work on clothing fashioned in Asia for brand labels so that the finished products could be shipped out to the United States duty-free. The dozens of factories that were quickly built contributed significantly to the revenues that were used to improve infrastructure and government services. By 1997, there were 34 garment factories in the Northern Marianas employing some 16,000 foreign workers (Stewart 2011). The numbers associated with this industry were impressive. "At the industry's apex in 1999, the plants exported US$1.07 billion worth of garments to the US and paid about US$79 million in taxes and fees into the CNMI treasury, about 35% of total public revenues" (Quimby 2013, 470). The garment industry, through the additional revenue it generated, certainly helped make the islands more attractive, even if it could not be regarded as the key element in the rise and fall of tourism.

In all, tourism expansion continued on through the 1990s until it reached its height in 1997, the year in which CNMI recorded 726,000 visitors. The previous decade or two had been a time of rapid hotel development and very fast growth in visitor numbers. In the 20 years between 1978 and 1997, the number of visitors had grown ninefold. Few would have expected the Northern Marianas to reach within striking distance of Guam's total, as it had done. Indeed, the Marianas Visitors Authority and local boosters were already poised to cut the cake for the celebration as the annual visitor number reached one million.

PEAK YEARS OF TOURISM

By the mid-1990s, Saipan had blossomed into a tourist wonderland. The island offered a variety of activities and tourist sites for Japanese and the increasing number of other visitors who vacationed on the island. Tour agencies offered trips to the Grotto, a 50-foot-deep natural cavern fed by the ocean, and to nearby Bird Island. There were boats to carry visitors to Managaha Island for swimming and picnicking, a submarine for those wishing to explore the underwater world of the lagoon, and dive shops to provide services for tourists who preferred scuba diving and snorkeling tours. Travel agents offered those visitors who might be interested in more than just coral and fish the chance to visit the island's few underwater wrecks: a Japanese Zero fighter, a submarine, B-29 bomber, as well as the Japanese freighter *Shoun Maru* lying off Tinian. Saipan also offered parasailing, windsurfing, and catamaran cruises, including the popular sunset cruises with drinks and music. For those interested in getting away for a golf holiday, Saipan provided a choice of three golf courses: Marianas Country Club in the north, Saipan Country Club in Susupe, and Coral Ocean Point Country Club in the south.

 The island's historical monuments had special appeal to Japanese tourists, who still constituted the large majority of all visitors. Tours around the island included stops at the Last

As in the case of Japan, Koreans themselves provided much of the investment for their own market

Command Post in the north, where Japanese forces offered their final resistance to invading US forces, and to the spots where hundreds of Japanese civilians jumped to their death: Suicide Cliff overlooking the northern plain, and Banzai Cliff fronting the northern shore of the island. At these sites, visitors could pay reverence to war casualties at the shrines erected by Japanese donors. On Tinian, which then was linked to Saipan by regular ferry service and a small aircraft, tourists could visit the pits on North Field at which the atomic bombs were loaded onto the B-29s that dropped them on Hiroshima and Nagasaki, and guests could see the giant limestone pillars at the famed latte stone site known as the House of Taga. The historical points of interest included not just wartime monuments, but reminders of the prosperous days under the Japanese occupation, and even local traditional sites highlighting island culture.

The scale of hotel expansion during this period can be gauged by the rapid escalation in the number of rooms for visitors. Saipan, which offered only 100 rooms back in 1970, finally reached the 1,000-room mark in 1986, and within just three more years, by 1989, the number of rooms had doubled to over 2,000. By 1998, just after the peak of the tourist boom, the number had grown to 4,600 (Table 1).

The booming tourist industry, as economist Bill Stewart writes, supported more than hotel construction and operations. It also gave rise to a wide variety of businesses that would respond to the needs of visitors. "Restaurants, souvenir vendors, handicraft producers, automobile rental agencies, service stations, travel agencies, dive shops and ground tour agents were examples of the many businesses which opened on Saipan, very many of which were owned and operated by Asian investors" (Stewart 2011).

As the industry expanded, it no longer centered quite as exclusively on the town of Garapan as it once did. In earlier years, during the 1970s and early 1980s, many of the new hotels were situated there. Soon there were shopping centers catering to Asian tourists, one of the most popular of which was Duty Free Galleria. Another was built by the local businessman Joe Tenorio near the greatly expanded Hafadai Hotel. With the opening of new stores and shopping malls and eateries in the area, Garapan quickly became a tourist mecca—something of a replica of the populous, busy community it had been in the 1930s under the Japanese. By the late 1980s, however, the tourist boom began to affect other parts of the island as well. Two large luxury hotels and a new shopping mall were built in the San Roque area, even as other hotels were opened in the southern part of the island. By the early 1990s tourism embraced the entire western side of Saipan.

As tourism grew—alongside the fledgling garment industry—so did the resident population of Saipan. In just five years, the census showed an increase of over 15,000 residents. The 1995 census recorded a total population in the CNMI of 58,846 representing an increase of 36 percent over the 1990 population of 43,345 (CNMI 1997). This reflected the rapid increase in foreign workers recruited for both tourism and the garment industry. The fast-paced growth of tourism made it inevitable that the number of jobs produced would outstrip the capacity of the local population to handle the labor requirements. This meant that foreign labor had to be brought in, largely from the Philippines, to man the hotels and other businesses. In 1995, the tourism industry directly employed 9,600 persons, only 2,700 of whom were local residents (Quimby 2013, 468). By that same year, local people (those of Chamorro or Carolinian ethnicity) represented only 34.3 percent of the total population in the Northern Marianas (CNMI 1997). The population increase in the Northern Marianas, prompted in part by the sudden rise of tourism, had been going on for some

Garapan quickly became a tourist mecca—something of a replica of the populous, busy community it had been in the 1930s under the Japanese

years by that time. From just 14,519 people in 1980, the population rose to 58,846 by 1995, even as the percentage of Chamorro and Carolinian people was steadily shrinking (CNMI 1997).

Whatever the drawbacks of tourism, its economic impact on the islands was pronounced. The revenue internally generated in the Northern Marianas rose from $58.3 million in 1985 to $203.6 million in 1995 (Stewart 2011, Table 4). Admittedly, not all of this increase resulted from tourism, but much of it certainly did. This added revenue translated into greater earnings for the people of the Northern Marianas. Between 1980 and 1990 per capita income jumped from $2,418 to $7,199 (CNMI 1997). Even though the figure dipped to $6,984 between 1990 and 1995, the decline is attributed to an increase in the number of nonresident workers, primarily in the garment industry.[10] For those longtime residents of the island not working at the minimum wage, however, it was a time of seemingly endless prosperity.

FIRST SLUMP (1997–2002)

Just as tourism in the Northern Marianas was soaring and seemed to have unlimited growth potential for the future, the Asian economic crisis struck in 1997. Japan, which had roamed the world for several years looking for real estate and development projects in which to invest its newfound wealth, was caught unawares as the Japanese investment bubble burst. The crash of the Japanese market affected its Asian neighbors as well, as visitor figures for the Northern Marianas show. In a single year, between 1997 and 1998, Japan's visitors dropped by 54,000, while the number of visitors from Korea plunged 77 percent, from 169,000 to 39,000 (Table 2). To compound the problem, a Korean Airlines plane crashed on Guam that same year, leading to the abrupt pullout by Korean Airlines of all flights to Guam and Saipan (MVA 2006, 14). Overall, the number of visitors plunged from 726,000 to 526,000 during the period—a drop of 28 percent.

> The number of visitors plunged from 726,000 to 526,000 during the period—a drop of 28 percent

These disasters had a downward-spiral effect on the Northern Marianas. Hotel construction and other projects were suddenly halted and real estate sold off. Establishments all over Saipan that catered to Koreans all but lost their businesses (MVA 2006, 14). The repercussions on the island economy were significant; within a single year island business had dropped 15 percent. "Business gross revenues, which peaked at US$2.6 billion in 1997, declined by US$400 million to US$2.2 billion in 1998," Quimby writes (2013, 469).

The following years brought new problems—the terrorist attacks of September 2001 and the SARS epidemic of 2003. By comparison with the Asian financial crisis, the terrorist skyjacking and attacks of 9/11 were nothing more than a blip on the screen for tourism in the Northern Marianas. The number of Japanese visitors, already in decline because of the financial crisis, dipped in 2002 but soon began a slow climb until the next slump hit in 2006. Korean visitor numbers dropped off following the SARS epidemic, but by 2006 the Korean market was once again on an upward trend (Table 2). US visitor numbers had been falling steadily since 1995, and their number has continued to drop up to the present, in part as a consequence of the reduced air service to and from Saipan, especially on flights from Guam (MVA 2012, 51).

In mid-2001, something else happened that would eventually have a much greater impact on tourism than any of the other problems occurring at that time. A series of legal battles began over Article XII in the Constitution of the Commonwealth of the Northern Marianas. The issue in question was the interpretation of the land alienation clauses that expressly stated that only people of Northern Marianas descent can own land and all others must lease for no longer than 55 years (MVA 2006, 13). Despite the efforts of the CNMI government to take measures that might restore the confidence of foreign investors, a series of highly publicized legal cases came to court. Consequently, several Japanese investments were halted and earlier land agreements put in peril.[11] Within a few years the tourist industry would feel the full effects of this land issue.

Meanwhile, total visitor arrivals fell from 726,000 in 1997 to 424,000 in 2002, dropping by 300,000 in five years. Hardest hit were the Japanese and Korean markets, the mainstays of tourism in the Northern Marianas. Over the next three years (2002–2005) the tourist industry wavered, but showed no real decline; the number of visitors in 2005 was 529,000, nearly the same as the 1998 figure. But 2005 was the last year to show half a million visitors; each year since then has been substantially below that level.

SECOND SLUMP (2006–2011)

The tourism industry was just showing signs of stabilizing from its first serious downturn when a second slump began in 2006. It was triggered when Japan Air Lines (JAL) stopped its flights to the Marianas in October of the previous year. The airline had been suffering huge losses throughout its system, but it had special cause to terminate its service to the Marianas. Underwriting some of the hotels on Saipan, JAL saw its investments threatened by the court decisions that were then being handed down on Article XII in the Covenant of the CNMI. The specter of land leases being overturned when the paint was barely dry on the newly built hotels was enough to frighten off any serious investor.

Suspension of JAL air service to the Marianas was a severe blow to the tourist industry. The airline had been operating 14 flights a week to Saipan, and it transported more than half of the 400,000 Japanese tourists visiting the island annually (MVA 2012, 13). JAL's departure meant the loss of an invaluable partner in promoting tourism in the Northern Marianas' biggest market and shut down some of the largest tourist projects. Not long after the airline's departure, Saipan saw the closure of the La Fiesta San Roque Shopping Center, a $60 million development owned by JAL. The airline also closed its Saipan-based tour bus company and eventually sold the JAL-owned Hotel Nikko Saipan, which thereafter lost its international brand-name marketing in Japan (MVA 2012, 13).

Japanese visitors, who had numbered 450,000 in 1997, soon dropped to barely 200,000, and in recent years the number has dipped much lower (Table 2). The damage to Marianas tourism would have been even more catastrophic if Northwest Airlines had not stepped in and increased its service between Japan and the islands.[12] Even so, the yearly overall visitor total dropped to a low of 338,000 in 2011 before the numbers slowly began to recover (Table 1).

As the number of visitors fell, hotels were shut down. The largest losses occurred on Saipan, which saw the closure of two large hotels, the 114-room Plumeria Resort in 2009 and the 313-room Palms Resort in 2010 (MVA 2012, 94). But the smaller islands in the Northern Marianas suffered as well.

Accommodations on the island of Rota dropped from 11 hotels to seven. The Rota Pau Pau Hotel, with 50 rooms was the first to close, followed by several

2005 was the last year to show half a million visitors; each year since then has been substantially below that level

small, locally-owned properties. Tinian lost one small locally-owned establishment, the 14-room Tinian Hotel (MVA Report 2012, 94).

Those hotels that did not close were forced to cut back services in the face of declining occupancy rates in an effort to weather this latest storm. An assessment of the situation in 2012
by the Marianas Visitors Authority reported:

> Luxury accommodations are very limited, and there are no true five-star accom-
> modations in the destination at this time. As fallout from the prolonged downturn
> in visitor arrivals, most hotels in the Northern Marianas have experienced major
> challenges, if not sustained financial losses (MVA 2012, 93).

The Northern Marianas also experienced the shut-down of the garment industry in 2006
after international trade agreements the year before lifted the quotas on worldwide apparel
export. The billion-dollar business, which was built on the advantage it enjoyed thanks to its
duty-free and quota-free status, quickly crumbled as the 34 garment factories on Saipan were
closed one after another. US federal authorities took this opportunity to bring the Northern
Marianas in line with national standards on immigration quotas and procedures, besides which
they began implementing the US minimum wage in the commonwealth. This had the effect of
worsening the financial shock resulting from the closing down of the garment industry and
the pullout by JAL and other Japanese investors.

The result was a fiscal crisis for the Northern Marianas—a period that residents and
outside observers agreed was "the worst time in CNMI history" (Quimby 2013, 464). "The
major economic downturn," in the words of the same author, "was deepened and prolonged
by the global recession. The depressed economy severely reduced government revenues,
challenged the CNMI's capacity to provide essential public services and caused a painful
decline in the islands' standard of living" (Quimby 2013, 464). This, in turn, led to a major
exodus of temporary foreign workers as well as local islanders who sought employment
elsewhere.

The financial condition of the Northern Marianas government seriously weakened as its
economy shrank to half of what it had been.

> The islands' GDP, which had peaked in 1997 at US$1.5 billion, declined 49%—
> US$1.2 billion to US$598 million—from 2002 to 2009. The CNMI's accumulated
> deficit grew from US$50 million in 1998 to US$316 million at the end of fiscal
> year 2010. CNMI government revenues declined from about US$213 million in
> 2001 to US$137 million in 2009 (Quimby 2013, 479).

The drop in tourism and the loss of Saipan's garment industry led to an enormous drop in
resources available to the Northern Marianas government. From a peak of $247 million in
1997 the government budget plunged to just $102 million in 2012 (MVA 2012, ix). This drop
meant that the government would be hard-pressed to maintain public services, provide funds for
the upkeep of tourist sites, and support the tourist promotion that would be needed to restore
the tourism industry. In other words, the Northern Marianas had not only suffered devastating

losses, but it was without the resources it needed to revitalize the single industry that might drive its economy in the years ahead.

ON THE ROAD TO RECOVERY (2012–PRESENT)

Visitors to the Northern Marianas, who numbered 726,000 in 1997, the high-water mark of the tourism boom, fell to a low of 338,000 in 2011. Since then the number of visitors has shown healthy growth by over 100,000 during the most recent three years, reaching 479,000 in 2015 (Table 1). Although the number of visitors from Japan continues to dwindle, the growth of the new Chinese market has spurred this latest recovery.

Tourism from mainland China began slowly during the late 1990s with just a couple thousand visitors a year, but it has exploded in the last four years. Between 2012 and 2014, the number of visitors from China nearly doubled, from 79,000 to 157,000 (Table 2). The number increased by another 15 percent in 2015. Today the Chinese market (at 38 percent of all visitors) has surpassed the Japanese market and is neck and neck with Korea as the largest component of tourism in the Northern Marianas (Daleno 2015). With good reason, then, China is regarded by the Northern Marianas as the main prospect for the future, especially in view of its nearly unlimited growth potential. Currently, three airlines are providing regular service from China: China Eastern Airlines, Dynamic Airways, and Sichuan Airways (MVA 2012, 89).

The Korean market dropped substantially between 1997 and 1998—from about 170,000 to 40,000—as a result of the economic crisis. But Korean numbers have increased steadily over the past years until the market has entirely regained the ground lost: Korean visitors were up to a new high of 181,000 in 2015 (Table 2). As other markets have declined, Korea is claiming an ever greater share of the total visitors—from 17 percent of the total market in 2005 to 38 percent in 2015 (Daleno 2015). Stable air service has been an important part of the resurgence of this market. Asiana Airlines has been serving the market with two daily flights direct from Korea and other flights on four-day-a-week schedules, all originating out of Incheon/Seoul (MVA 2012, 22). Recently another airline, Jeju Air, has begun flights from Korea. Korean visitors have been granted visa-free entry to the Marianas in a concession approved by the US Department of Homeland Security.

Koreans are not only back in greater numbers, but they are investing in the Northern Marianas once again. Korean investors purchased the largest golf resort on Saipan in 2007, subsequently building a new hotel with luxury facilities that opened in 2009. Koreans have also invested in the largest waterpark hotel, Saipan World Resort, which was purchased in 2010. According to the MVA strategic plan, "Korean companies also own numerous office buildings, retail stores, restaurants and land tour companies" (MVA 2012, 22).

The United States was never as big or as promising a market as some of the Asian countries, although US visitors did reach 95,000 at its height in 1995 (Table 2). The number has steadily decreased since then, dropping to 19,244 in 2015—a number that includes Guam residents as well as travelers from the United States (MVA 2015). Part of the explanation for this decline may be the poor quality of air service between Guam and Saipan. Cape Air, the airline operating as Continental Express, had to cancel flights repeatedly because of mechanical problems (MVA 2012, 51). The Commonwealth made a couple of attempts to establish its own airline in recent years to counter the slump of its tourist industry. Fly Guam Airline, launched in 2011,

With good reason, then, China is regarded by the Northern Marianas as the main prospect for the future went out of business within a year. A second airline, Saipan Air, was announced the following year and has plans to serve Japan as well as other destinations (MVA 2012, 90). At present, as over the past decade or so, the assessment of the situation by the MVA stands: "Air service between Guam and Saipan is pricey and poor" (MVA 2012, 89).

With the steady drop in Japanese visitors to the Marianas, the market has never returned to what it once was. With its yearly visitor numbers hovering at around 150,000 between 2011 and 2013, Japan seemed poised to recover from its long decline. Instead, the visitor totals from Japan plunged to 88,000 for 2015 or 18 percent of the visitors for that year (Table 2). Currently two American carriers, Delta and United, are offering regular service to the Marianas, but Japan Airlines has never resumed its flights to Saipan. The lack of stable air service, a significant reduction in destination marketing, and the devaluation of the yen against the US dollar all contributed to the major decline in Japanese tourism.

Russian visitors began to appear on the scene in 2006, just as the second downturn was beginning. The number began slowly rising, with 11,000 visitors from Russia in 2013, leading to speculation that Russia might be another developing market. Since then, however, the number has dropped sharply. For some time now, at least one of the most popular hotels on Saipan (Pacific Islands Club) has been offering translations of its menu in Russian. At first Russian tourists would fly to Korea and then take Asiana Airlines, or to Japan and on to Saipan by Delta Airlines (MVA 2012, 44). However, there is now a direct service from Russia on two of its airlines: Aeroflot from Vladivostok and Yakutia Airlines from Khabarovsk (MVA 2012, 89).

For more than a decade, public and private stakeholders of the islands have marketed to attract Chinese and Russian tourists. These two markets present a major opportunity: China and Russia are recognized by leading international tourism organizations as the fastest growing outbound markets in the world (MVA 2012, 8). Although a permanent visa waiver has not yet been granted for Russians and Chinese, the United States has granted the Northern Marianas a "parole system," under which a temporary visa-free entry system is allowed for Chinese and Russian tourists. While this system is subject to change, it currently offers the Northern Marianas a significant competitive advantage over other destinations (MVA 2012, 34).

THE FUTURE

"No other Pacific island economy has experienced such an extreme degree of expansion and contraction since the Asian financial crisis of the late-1990s," one author noted without exaggeration (Quimby 2013, 479). The rapid rise and fall of the garment industry in the islands has certainly played a large part in this drama, as we have seen. Even so, the wild fluctuations in tourism during the islands' chase for a strong economic base over the past 40 years is a story in its own right.

The Northern Marianas took advantage of early opportunities to develop tourism based on Japanese visitors, lured by their sudden prosperity, their historical ties with the islands, and proximity to an island setting that offered plenty of sand, sea, and sunshine. Visitors from other Asian nations, such as Korea and more recently China, have flocked to the same destination for vacation. The Northern Marianas, with the advantages offered by its Covenant with the United States, was in a favorable position to respond. It welcomed the visitors with minimal fuss over visas, thanks to the exemption granted it by the United States. In addition, it gratefully received

For more than a decade, public and private stakeholders of the islands have marketed to attract Chinese and Russian tourists

the investments that these other nations were willing to make in expanding tourist capacity for its clientele, again because of tax exemptions and a liberal foreign-investment policy permitted by the United States. Yet, the essential factors governing the rapid decline of the tourist industry —especially the upheaval caused by the Asian financial crisis—were clearly beyond the control of the Northern Marianas. Tourism is an uncertain industry, as the islands learned from all this.

Despite the slump in recent years, Saipan still has 12 resorts and large hotels in operation. Two of these hotels feature waterparks, and three are golf resorts (MVA 2012, 93). Indeed, some of these facilities appear to have weathered the tourism drop-off by offering features that might prove attractive to resident families on the island. Most of the small hotels that housed tourists on Tinian and Rota during the boom days appear to have closed. As always, these two islands have been outliers of Saipan, living off the leftovers of an industry that has always been centered on much more-populous Saipan. Even the Dynasty Hotel on Tinian, opened in 1998 to entice visitors with a passion for casino gambling but nearly vacant throughout its years of operation, finally shut its doors in 2015.

Tourism, whatever its vicissitudes in the past, remains the hope of the Northern Marianas' economic future, if only because the island group has few options. No one holds any hope that the garment industry will be revived, and other forms of manufacturing are simply out of the question. Lack of resources, small population, and distance from major markets are prohibitive obstacles for the Northern Marianas as they are nearly everywhere in the Pacific.

Visitor figures for the first half of 2015 were encouraging. Monthly arrivals consistently surpassed the figures for the previous year, and the Northern Marianas seemed to be on pace to break the half-million visitor mark by the end of the fiscal year.[13] Then, in August, Typhoon Soudolur devastated Saipan, crippling the power-distribution system as it caused severe damage to roads and other infrastructure. With this, any hope for a rapid resurgence of the tourist industry faded.

Yet, the growing number of visitors from China is an encouraging sign for the future. As China's economy expands and the well-to-do population of that country increases, the Chinese are scouring the northwestern Pacific and Southeast Asia looking for vacation spots for the millions who can now easily afford what would have once been an unthinkable luxury. Chinese visitors are already having a striking impact on other places, including Palau. For the Northern Marianas, the Chinese market offers the promise of becoming the foundation of the tourist industry that the Japanese market had been for so long. Chinese firms are already investing in real estate and hotels on Saipan. One has already leased land in Garapan for the construction of a large new hotel of over 400 rooms, along with a full casino, for Chinese visitors.[14]

Meanwhile, the Korean market is expanding, even as the number of Japanese visitors shrinks by the year. The Russian market that tourist planners viewed so optimistically at first has never grown as expected; visitors for 2015 numbered no more than a few hundred a month. However fragile these other markets might seem, the Northern Marianas hopes to continue nurturing them even as Chinese tourism seems ready to explode. "We want to make sure the Chinese market will not overwhelm the other markets," the current president of the Saipan Chamber of Commerce warns (Daleno 2015).

Recent experience in the Northern Marianas has taught people the importance of balance: a balance between China and other markets, but a balance between other factors as well. There is a growing public consensus that "in place of the laissez faire expansion of the 1980s and

Tourism, whatever its vicissitudes in the past, remains the hope of the Northern Marianas' economic future

1990s" the Northern Marianas people maintain firm control of the pace and direction of the growth of their tourist industry. Only such control will balance "the need for foreign investment, local jobs and government revenue streams" with "quality of life, land alienation protections and government accountability" (Quimby 2013, 483).

REFERENCES

Ashman, Mike. 1974. "Micronesia Tastes Tourism," in *A New Kind of Sugar: Tourism in the Pacific*, eds. Ben Finney and Karen Ann Watson, 135–143. Honolulu: The East-West Center.

Central Intelligence Agency. 2015. "Northern Mariana Islands," *CIA World Factbook*.

CIA. *See* Central Intelligence Agency.

CNMI. *See* Commonwealth of the Northern Mariana Islands.

Commonwealth of the Northern Mariana Islands. 1997. *The CNMI Guide*. www.cnmi-guide .com/infos.

Daleno, Gaynor. 2015. "'Right Size' Of Saipan Casino Development Encouraged." *Pacific Islands Report*, June 25.

Hezel, Francis X. 1995. *Strangers in Their Own Land: A Century of Colonial Rule in the Caroline and Marshall Islands*. Pacific Islands Monograph Series no 13. Honolulu: University of Hawai'i Press.

Honolulu Advertiser. 1971a. Tourism Supplement. March 7.

———. 1971b. Tourism Supplement. December 29.

———. 1972. Tourism Supplement. January 31.

Marianas Visitors Authority. 1978–2015. "Visitor Arrival Statistics."

———. 2006. "Northern Mariana Islands Strategic Initiatives for 2006–2010." Prepared by the Ad Hoc Tourism Committee, Strategic Economic Development Council. Saipan.

———. 2012. *Northern Mariana Islands Tourism Master Plan 2012–2016*. Saipan.

MVA. *See* Marianas Visitors Authority.

Osman, Wali. 2003. *Commonwealth of the Northern Mariana Islands Economic Report: October 2003*. Honolulu: Bank of Hawai'i and East-West Center. http://www.eastwestcenter .org/fileadmin/resources/pidp/jcc/cnmi03.pdf.

Pacific Daily News. 1989. Supplement on Saipan Tourism. May 11.

Peattie, Mark. 1988. *Nanyo: The Rise and Fall of the Japanese in Micronesia, 1885–1945.* Pacific Islands Monograph Series 4. Honolulu: University of Hawai'i Press.

Phillips, Ken. 1986. "Anticipation." *Guam Business News*. August.

Quimby, Frank. 2013. "Northern Mariana Islands Since 1978." *Journal of Pacific History* 48.4: 464–483.

Stewart, William H. 2005. "The NMI's Recent Economic History." *Saipan Tribune*, May 18.

———. 2012. "A Brief Historical Review of 'Selected' Forces and Factors Which Have Impacted the Economy of the Northern Marianas." Paper presented at the First Marianas History Conference, June 14–16, 2012. Saipan, Northern Marianas. https://issuu.com/guampedia/docs/recent_history/1?e=1294219/5924649

Trust Territory Government. 1969. "Tourism Status Report for the Year January–December 1969." Saipan: Department of Resources and Development.

———. 1970. "Travel Information." Saipan: Department of Resources and Development. January.

TT. *See* Trust Territory Government.

US Department of State. 1971–1975. *Annual Report of the Trust Territory of the Pacific Islands.* Washington, DC: Government Printing Office.

NOTES

[1] For a good historical overview of the Japanese colonial period in the Northern Marianas, see Peattie 1988.

[2] For a brief account of the split of the Northern Marianas from the Trust Territory, see Hezel 1995, 335–337, and Quimby 2013, 465–466.

[3] Ken and Bob Jones, early entrepreneurs on Guam and the Northern Marianas, provided the investment in the hotel, which has long since closed. Today the Saipan World Resort stands at the site of the former hotel. See Stewart 2012, 119.

[4] Visitor figures for these years are to be found in the US Department of State's *Annual Report on the Administration of the Trust Territory of the Pacific Islands* for those years.

[5] Both hotels were planned and built as part of a bidding competition for the new airline route in the islands, historian Bill Stewart writes. Continental Hotel, of course, represented the airline of the same name, while the Intercontinental was constructed by Pan Am. See Stewart 2012, 119.

[6] The effort to remove this constraint against foreign investment was largely the result of the visionary work of David Sablan, a prominent Saipanese businessman, Bill Stewart reports (Stewart 2012, 119).

[7] In February 1976 the Marianas Visitors Bureau (MVB) was established as a nonprofit organization for promotion and development of tourism. Reorganized in 1994, the MVB was placed under the US Department of Commerce for purposes of administration and coordination. In June 1998 the "Marianas Visitors Authority Act of 1998" was signed into law, abolishing the MVB and establishing a new public corporation known as the Marianas Visitors Authority.

[8] Japan had been growing in wealth for the past two decades, but the country's prosperity was aided immensely when the United States, due to its huge trade deficits among other factors, devalued the dollar in relation to the Japanese yen. By the end of 1987, Stewart (2012, 118) writes, "the dollar had fallen by 54% against the yen. This had the effect of doubling the size of the Japanese economy almost overnight and was the 'kick-off' for massive amounts of Japanese investment in the NMI's tourism."

[9] An article on the new airport mentions that its completion is especially timely because of Air Micronesia's expansion of routes to Australia and Bali just a month before (*Pacific Daily News* 1989).

[10] The minimum wage in the Commonwealth was $3.05 per hour, as of July 1997, for all sectors of the economy. The thousands of workers being hired in the garment industry during the early 1990s were reported as dragging down the average income CNMI 1997.

[11] For fuller details on the legal issues involved, see Quimby 2013, 472.

[12] Northwest Airlines, now known as Delta since the merger of the two airlines, continues to operate flights from Japan to Saipan. Meanwhile, JAL has resumed its flights to Saipan, although on a limited basis (Quimby 2013, 468–469; MVB 2012, 13).

[13] The data for monthly visitor arrivals are taken from monthly reports of the Marianas Visitors Authority, most of which were reissued in *Pacific Islands Report*, the website sponsored by Pacific Islands Development Program, East-West Center, Honolulu.

[14] Best Sunshine, the firm behind this venture, is finalizing leases and has architectural plans for the emporium that it hopes to have finished within two years (Daleno 2015).

Conclusion

DISTANCE RUN AFTER A HALF CENTURY

The three island groups chosen as case studies for this treatment of tourism have had a great deal in common. They shared a long colonial history, including three decades of Japanese rule. They also benefitted from the rapid development of the 1960s that resulted from an abrupt swing in US policy toward its trust territory. A major US carrier (Continental Airlines) began operations in the area near the end of that decade, making tourism viable for the first time. The island groups also had similar obstacles to overcome. After all, none of them had the hotels and other facilities needed for a successful tourist industry; none could offer any more than a few dozen hotel rooms in the late 1960s. It is unusual in the social sciences to have a set of historical circumstances that closely approximate a controlled experiment, but Chuuk, Palau, and the Northern Marianas all shared a common history as they began their chase of a tourist industry and all left the gate at the same time.

Chuuk, Palau, and the Northern Marianas all shared a common history as they began their chase of a tourist industry

Today, nearly a half century later, the results vary from one place to another. Palau, which began slowly but has grown steadily over the years, now shows over 160,000 visitors a year and already has 1,600 rooms, with new hotels under construction, to provide for the ever-increasing flow of visitors. The Northern Marianas, which showed astonishing early growth that peaked in 1997, dropped sharply for several years and has only begun to rebound in the past few years. It now hosts about 480,000 annual visitors and has 3,500 rooms. Chuuk, on the other hand, shares the fate of the rest of the FSM: tourism has never been a major factor in that island's economy. Chuuk entertains only about 6,000 visitors a year, comparable with the figure for Pohnpei, and offers about 140 rooms.

In Palau, as we have seen, the real growth of tourism began with the partnership between a Japanese investor and a few prominent Palauans that led to the opening in 1985 of the Palau Pacific Resort, still the island's premier hotel today. The Japanese market played a leading role in the development of tourism in its earliest days and Japanese numbers have expanded over the years. Other Asian countries, especially Taiwan and China, have also contributed greatly in recent years. Although its thriving tourism industry has become the heart of Palau's economy, the small island nation has taken measures to limit the inflow of tourists, especially as the number of visitors from China explodes. Palau is one of the few tourist destinations to attempt to cut back on its tourism industry (Oceania TV 2015).

The Northern Marianas was off to a quick start in building its tourism, thanks to a large Japanese market. Japanese and Americans comprised just about all of its visitors until a growing number of Korean tourists were added to the mix beginning in the late 1980s. After reaching a high of 700,000 visitors in 1997, tourism experienced a sharp decline. Visitor numbers plummeted in the late 1990s because of the Asian financial crisis and dipped again in 2007 for other reasons. Tourism there only started to recover in 2011, due in great part to a large increase in Korean and Chinese mainland visitors.

Chuuk, which experienced a promising beginning in 1970 with the opening of the Continental Hotel and the discovery of wreck diving, never saw its tourism grow appreciably over the years. The number of visitors increased modestly throughout that first decade, but has remained unchanged since then. Wreck diving still draws a handful of enthusiasts each week, but tourism has never met the high expectations of its early years. It has proven insignificant as a source of revenue for the state.

KEY FACTORS IN TOURISM DEVELOPMENT

The lure of a lucrative tourist industry that can jump-start an economy with little else to depend on is understandably strong for Pacific Island nations. Yet, not every island nation can generate this type of tourism, as we have seen. Palau has a burgeoning tourist market that is expected to grow in coming years, and the Northern Marianas has more than double the number of visitors Palau receives each year. Chuuk, on the other hand, has barely 6,000 visitors a year. Moreover, its neighbors have been no more successful than Chuuk: The entire Federated States of Micronesia has just 20,000 visitors a year, and the Marshall Islands has less than half that number (Hezel 2012, 16). What, then, explains the success of some island groups and the failure of others?

Many places in the Pacific offer "sun, sea, and sand" to tourists looking for a vacation spot. A healthy tourist industry clearly depends on much more than the natural features of the island group. Success depends on natural assets and other attractions, good planning, ready response to outside investment opportunities, and local initiative; but it also may be a result of serendipity or dumb luck. Here we will review what appear to have been the key factors in determining the outcome of the attempts of these three Micronesian island groups to establish tourism.

What explains the success of some island groups and the failure of others?

Location

All three of the island groups are relatively close to the large Asian markets, upon which successful tourism in Micronesia has come to depend. The United States market, as the tourist figures reveal, has been of minor significance in the area; Australia and New Zealand, too, have been inconsequential. Asian visitors have been the mainstay of the tourist industry up to now and will very likely continue to be such in the future.

Northern Marianas enjoys an especially favorable location thanks to its proximity to the major Asian countries as well as to Guam, the transportation hub of the western Pacific. During the 1970s, Saipan was able to exploit this advantage to develop a growing tourism industry. Even today visitors can purchase a round-trip ticket to Saipan from Tokyo, Seoul, or Beijing for the comparatively low fare of $1,000 or less (Table 1).

Although the onset of tourism in Palau was delayed a decade, its location close to mainland Asia represented an enormous advantage. When Air Nauru first introduced flights between Palau and Manila over 30 years ago, a link was established with Southeast Asia—especially Indonesia, Thailand, the Philippines, and later Vietnam—that offered tourists the opportunity for a package vacation with stops in multiple destinations. A Japanese businessman, when recently asked why he was investing in land in Palau, sketched a rough map of the island group with two circles drawn around it, one representing a flying time of four hours and the other a five-hour flight (Jennifer Gibbons interview). As he scribbled the names of major Asian cities

Table 1. Cost of Economy Round-trip Airfares from Major Asian Cities

Country	Capital	Tokyo	Seoul	Beijing
American Samoa	PagoPago	$1,800	$1,873	$2,305
CNMI	Saipan	$575	$732	$1,047
Cook Islands	Raratonga	$6,103	$1,794	$2,810
Fiji	Nadi	$1,153	$1,646	$1,300
French Polynesia	Papeete	$2,683	$2,710	$3,491
Guam	Agana	$498	$497	$822
Kiribati	Tarawa	$3,832	$2,410	$3,671
Marshall Islands	Majuro	$1,915	$923	$1,642
Micronesia	Pohnpei	$1,389	$1,064	$1,412
Nauru	Nauru	$2,101	$2,594	$2,248
New Caledonia	Noumea	$1,288	$1,603	$1,819
Palau	Koror	$989	$1,135	$1,445
Papua New Guinea	Port Moresby	$1,229	$1,791	$1,851
Samoa	Apia	$1,514	$1,641	$2,767
Solomon Islands	Honiara	$1,505	$2,075	$1,767
Timor-Leste	Dili	$2,025	$1,429	$1,345
Tonga	Tonga	$1,602	$1,834	$2,826
Tuvalu	Funafuti	$1,769	$2,262	$1,916
Vanuatu	Port Vila	$1,225	$2,156	$2,260

Sources:
Travelocity, United Airlines sites as of October 29, 2015.

within the outer radius, the comparative advantage enjoyed by Palau became obvious. How many other Pacific tourist destinations are within such easy reach of Tokyo, Taipei, Hong Kong, Manila, Seoul, Shanghai, Singapore, and Hanoi?

Chuuk, along with Pohnpei and the rest of the FSM, adds enough flying time and cost to an Asian visitor's ticket to raise second thoughts about making it a destination. Some 20 years ago an FSM tourism official explained that it was more expensive to fly from Guam to Chuuk (roughly an hour and a half flying time) than it was to get from Japan to Guam (a flight of more than three hours). Even today an economy flight from Tokyo to Saipan costs less than half of what a flight from Tokyo to Chuuk would cost (Table 1).

Link to a Start-Up Market

A successful tourist industry in this part of the Pacific seems to grow out of a strong link with at least one Asian nation. Clearly, the takeoff of tourism in Palau and the Northern Marianas was reliant on attracting a growing Japanese market. This could be seen as fortuitous since Japan was enjoying its newfound national prosperity just as tourism was opening up in the islands. Japanese might have been attracted to those two island groups because of their proximity, but there were other reasons as well. Historical and cultural ties dating from the Japanese colonial era and World War II may have also contributed to Japanese interest. All three spots in Micronesia had long familiarity with Japanese culture and language, and all provided historical sites that served as reminders of these ties.

Saipan, as we have seen, offered an abundance of historical monuments—not just buildings and structures in town, but military sites as well. Palau offered the same: Koror, the town that Japanese civilian government had built in prewar days, as well as Peleliu and Angaur, where thousands of Japanese troops had died in the final year of the war. Japanese who wanted to relax on the beach could do so, but within the ambience of the familiar. Whether in Palau or on Saipan, they could make jaunts to visit historical sites. In Palau, they might visit the building that once housed the administration of the Japanese mandate, or the old Nanyo Boeki store, or walk along Geisha Lane. On Saipan, the visitor could find the statue of the Japanese entrepreneur who established the sugar industry in the islands, the ruins of a Japanese elementary school, and the old airport.

In Chuuk, which had once been under the same Japanese colonial rule, such monuments were much less easy to find. The administrative center of Chuuk under Japanese rule was situated on Tonoas, an island a few miles removed from Weno, the present commercial and government center. Even on Tonoas, relics were scarce—perhaps because of the fury of a US commander at the end of the war who destroyed as much of the Japanese infrastructure as he could (Hezel 1995, 250–251). The most remarkable and vivid reminder of the Japanese era lay 100 feet or more below the surface of the Chuuk lagoon: the wrecks of the Japanese vessels sunk in the US air attacks during the final year of the war. To explore these monuments, however, visitors would have to don masks and tanks to dive the sunken fleet.

Such historical reminders of a shared past may seem of little consequence in the long run, but they, along with the ticket price, might well have influenced the choice of destination during the initial spurt of Japanese visitors. Whatever the case, Japanese tourists did come in numbers and so founded the tourism industry in Palau and Saipan.

To be sure, the dynamic of tourism is such that once a place is recognized as an established tourist destination, the initial cultural attractions might fade in importance without harming the industry. Later visitors from other markets—Korean, Taiwanese, or Chinese—would not expect to find reflections of their own colonial heritage in the islands they visit, of course. But for the Japanese, the pioneer tourists in these islands, the importance of such reminders of their own stamp on the islands they visited cannot be discounted.

Air Service

Airline service to a destination generally follows rather than anticipates public demand, as airline executives are very quick to point out. Yet, there are critical contributions that an airline can make in generating tourism: It can provide the foundational service to a potential destination, and it can promote a destination through its own advertising.

Continental Airlines set up flights throughout the region when it replaced Pan Am in 1968, even as it immediately established a link with Honolulu and points east. Before long it did the same with key Asian cities via Guam. With the arrival of Air Micronesia, a subsidiary of Continental Airlines, the basic air service was in place for a tourism industry; this would be expanded as the number of visitors increased from place to place. The airline not only provided regular air service to the region, but within two years of its arrival it built hotels on four islands, including the three covered in this study.

Historical reminders of a shared past might well have influenced the choice of Japanese visitors

Its promotional efforts were significant as well. "Feel the Warmth of Paradise" was the theme, and it was reflected in the design on the tail of the planes ("The Proud Bird with the Golden Tail") as well as in the colorful uniforms of flight attendants. Continental did extensive marketing for all the islands it served—Chuuk as much as Palau and Saipan. Indeed, its pilots and flight crew made up a significant portion of the early wreck-diving enthusiasts in Chuuk. Continental's promotional efforts were also of critical importance in opening up the Taiwan market for Palau 20 years later, as we have seen.

Other airlines offered supportive roles during those early years. Air Nauru may have been short-lived, but it played a critical role in the development of Palau's tourist industry. Its flight service between Palau and Manila in 1982 was the first direct flight to Asia and provided easy access to labor from the Philippines as Palau's tourism industry was growing.[1] This was followed by direct flights between Palau and other Asian cities on other carriers. Air Nauru also experimented back in the late 1980s with a cheap flight through the FSM that included a stop in Chuuk. Although these innovations soon came to a halt, they assisted in the development of tourism in the region.

As the tourist flow increased in Palau and the Northern Marianas, charter flights were initiated as an important trial step while carriers experimented with the flow of the traffic and the durability of the market. In most cases these charter flights led to the establishment of regularly scheduled flights from Asian cities, most notably Taipei and Seoul. The most significant exception is Japan Airlines, which still operates on a charter basis today.

Availability of Land

In each of the three island groups studied, lease land was available as the tourism industry developed. Even in Chuuk, notorious for its land squabbles, the Continental Hotel was built on leased land with little difficulty. As it turned out, the Continental Hotel seemed to experience few problems until the airline eventually sold it to a Chuukese family interest. Land was much scarcer there than in other island groups because of Chuuk's size and population density, but local businessmen always seemed ready to provide the land needed for joint ventures.[2] Saipan was especially fortunate in that much of the middle section of the island, including Garapan, which would become the hub of the tourism industry, was government-owned since the end of World War II.

Determining just who has legal title to what piece of land is a problem everywhere in Micronesia, but it does not seem to be a decisive factor in tourism growth. After all, resolution of land disputes is as much an issue in Palau, notwithstanding its rapid growth, as in Chuuk. Years ago, the Palau government made it known that it would resolve outstanding land cases as speedily as possible so that prospective investors would know who has title to the land.[3] Yet, with 7,000 land cases still pending court judgment today, prospective investors in Palau are looking either for public land or land under the control of one of two prominent families. At a time of rapidly growing visitor numbers and ever-greater demand for additional hotel rooms, few investors are prepared to wait until a disputed land title is resolved.

Palau offers an enlightening example of how investors, in collaboration with local partners, could work around land difficulties and other related problems. The method successfully employed by the Japanese investor in putting up the first major hotel, Palau Pacific Resort, was to work with one or two influential Palauans to buy up the private land needed. This was

Continental did extensive marketing for all the islands it served—Chuuk as much as Palau and Saipan

expensive since it entailed paying two or three claimants for each piece of property required. It also took years to accomplish. Later, investors found that they could short-circuit this process by building on the tiny island of Malakal at the tip of Koror where virtually all the land is public under the authority of Koror State. The foreign investor would simply partner with an influential Palauan, who would then walk the application through the offices and bring back approval for the construction in a surprisingly short time.

Most investors today seem to be working through a single Palauan who either holds title to the land they require for the business or can easily acquire it through personal and family connections. This is allowing entrepreneurs today to avoid Malakal, which is becoming crowded, and utilize other parts of the island for constructing new tourist facilities. With land leases now extended from 25 years to 99 years, there is no need to maintain the type of long-term partnership between the Japanese investors and their Palauan counterparts that was so crucial in putting up the Palau Pacific Resort. Renegotiation of leases, after all, is no longer a major concern for the investor. Today's partnerships between Asian investors and Palauans are short-term marriages of convenience that are easily dissolved once the land is acquired and the construction is complete.

Like the other Micronesian nations nearby, Palau remains adamantly opposed to allowing the outright sale of land to foreigners, notwithstanding the advice it sometimes receives from international financial organizations to liberalize its land policies. Perhaps permitting long-term leases serves as a compromise measure. With the growth of tourism, the maximum land lease was extended at first from 25 to 50 years, and more recently to 99 years. These extensions have been helpful in gaining the confidence of investors, even if they were enacted by the national legislature for reasons that had little to do with tourism (US DOS 2013).

In the Northern Marianas, on the other hand, the problems were quite different. Large plots of land were available from the beginning, there seemed to be little confusion on land ownership, and long-term leases were easily offered to outside corporate investors to build the new hotels that were rising everywhere during the late 1980s and early 1990s. This liberal land-use policy was suddenly reversed, however, when an article of the constitution was invoked that restricted land ownership to local people and limited land leases to 55 years. Rather than gradually extending land leases in response to investment needs as Palau did, the Northern Marianas moved in the opposite direction. The effect was a loss of confidence on the part of foreign investors and disruption in the industry, although the tempest passed and tourism is on the rise there once again.

Only in the FSM have land-lease limits remained unchanged at 25 years. While short land leases remain a disincentive for foreign investment, legislation could be introduced to lengthen leases if the need ever arose, as happened in Palau.

Rapid Response to Economic Opportunities

We should note that none of the three island groups studied had all the elements in place to grow a successful tourist industry at the outset. It would appear from the history of tourism growth in these island groups that the final outcome was affected more by the ready response of the society and its government to opportunities and challenges presented.

The Northern Marianas has faced several challenges in recent years. In 2001, as the court battles began over the legality of the land agreements for hotels, the government somehow

Like the other Micronesian nations nearby, Palau remains adamantly opposed to allowing the outright sale of land to foreigners

managed to win back the confidence of Asian investors despite the earlier damage. Although Japanese carriers never returned, other airlines opened routes between Japanese cities and Saipan. Then, in 2006, when its garment industry was shut down and its economy crippled, the Northern Marianas shifted to an economy almost entirely dependent on tourism. The government used its own scant resources for the upkeep of tourist sites and did the promotional work needed for a resurgence of tourism. Then, as the market shifted from Japan to China and (briefly) Russia, the Northern Marianas petitioned the United States for a visa waiver to facilitate entry of visitors from these nations.

Chuuk might not have been presented with the many opportunities that the other islands groups enjoyed, but it did respond positively on a few occasions. When the first of the dive ships requested a business license in 1986, for instance, Chuuk found a way to modify the legal requirement that all commercial ventures have some local ownership so as to grant the ship its permit.

Palau has consistently shown a readiness to alter its course suddenly while building a national economy for itself. If one route toward development has been blocked, it has moved quickly to try another rather than remain at a dead end and wait in vain for the obstacles to be removed. Not all Pacific Island governments have shown the same resilience.

In the late 1990s, Palau had experimented with offshore banking; it had ten registered banks in operation between 1998 and 2001. This experiment came to a quick end when a senior US official met with the President of Palau to suggest that this offshore banking, because of its link to money laundering, could put Palau on a collision course with the United States (Hezel 2012, 15). When the banks were closed, Palau returned with renewed energy to developing its tourism industry, which expanded during the early years of the new century despite the overall contraction of tourism worldwide.

A few years later it became clear that the sale of fishing-license fees, which proved such an economic boon to some of its neighbors (especially to the FSM), was not going to provide significant revenue for Palau. At this the government took a new direction by declaring itself a shark sanctuary and an environmental haven. Besides attracting global attention and garnering funds from Green organizations, this move provided an additional important dimension for the tourism industry by adding ecotours to the long list of other attractions. The shift away from commercial fishing to developing the Palau National Marine Sanctuary bore quick results. In 2013, fishing-license fees brought in only $2.5 million, while visitor fees to Jellyfish Lake and the Rock Islands produced $7.5 million in revenue for that year (Jennifer Gibbons interview).

In response to years of public lobbying, the Palau congress modified the Foreign Investment Act in 2010. Foreign investors were no longer banned from those formerly protected businesses —such as tour guide, fishing guide, diving guide, water transportation, and travel and tour agency businesses—providing they established a partnership with a Palauan citizen (US DOS 2013). The results of this initiative were mixed, we might note. While the net effect of the legislation was to encourage outside investment in response to the heavy need for new tourist facilities, the legislation also gave rise to the "front" companies—financed by foreigners but headed by Palauans—that have become the new vehicles of tourist development today (US DOS 2013).

Palau has consistently shown a readiness to alter its course suddenly while building a national economy for itself

No Sure Formula

In this section we have tried to extract from the brief histories of tourism in these three island groups those factors that may have played a key role in the growth of the tourist industry in Micronesia. Tropical weather and good beaches are an important beginning, but only that. Reasonable access to a major market is another important feature needed. Reliable airline service, along with the promotional advertising that the airline provides, is an added advantage, but the case studies show that airline service normally increases in response to the growth in the number of visitors. A startup market—Japan, in the case of the Northern Marianas and Palau—was a critical element—although markets will almost always change in time as economic conditions fluctuate in the region.

Needless to say, the development of tourist facilities demands that land readily be made available for use. The land in question need not be owned outright by the foreign investors, but land leases must be of sufficient length to repay the initial investment. Most tourist destinations will modify their land policies accordingly, as we have seen. Even as they do so in response to the demands of foreign investors, however, they find that the bond between outside entrepreneurs and local facilitators becomes more utilitarian and less enduring than ever before.

More important than anything, tourist development depends on an island nation sustaining a productive relationship with those outside forces—investors, airlines, businessmen—who are prepared to offer their partnership in the growth of the tourist industry. This does not mean having everything firmly in place from the start, but it does imply a readiness to make necessary changes in business regulations as need demands.

These factors, while critical, certainly do not guarantee that tourism will succeed in an island nation. Chuuk, like other islands in the FSM, possessed most of these characteristics, but its tourism has been stunted almost from the beginning. It would seem that serendipity plays a much greater role in the success of tourist destinations than most economists and planners would like to admit. Pacific Island nations without other marketable resources can lay the groundwork for tourism and hope that eventually it will provide a badly needed engine for their island economies. But in the end, we can offer no sure formula for tourism development.

> Serendipity plays a much greater role in the success of tourist destinations than most economists and planners would like to admit

PROSPECTS FOR TOURISM IN THE PACIFIC

Tourism may be the fond hope of small Pacific Island nations with scant resources and few alternatives, but not all island nations enjoy a vibrant tourist industry at present. Indeed, the blessings of tourism are scattered unequally throughout the Pacific. According to Table 2, the total number of visitors to all Pacific island groups was 1.7 million. The island groups listed even include a pair of French territories, New Caledonia and French Polynesia, to round out the map of Oceania.[4] Yet, two islands alone—Guam and Saipan (CNMI)—neither listed in the table, had more visitors that same year than the rest of the Pacific combined. Together these two islands welcomed more than 1.8 million visitors in 2014 (Table 3). Both Guam and Saipan are situated north of the equator and reasonably close to mainland Asia; neither of them is an independent nation. Both are witness to the enormous disparity in tourism throughout the region.

Among the other Pacific nations, Fiji stands well in front of the rest with a total of 690,000 visitors in 2014. This represents one half of all the visitors to the entire Pacific, less the French and American territories (New Caledonia, French Polynesia, CNMI, and Guam). Fiji is blessed

Table 2. Pacific Islands, Population, and Visitors in 2014

Country	Population	Visitors (2014)
American Samoa	56,400	14,211
Cook Islands	15,300	121,462
Fiji	867,000	692,630
FSM	102,300	25,502
French Polynesia	285,200	180,602
Kiribati	113,400	1,401
Marshall Islands	54,900	2,269
New Caledonia	266,000	107,187
Niue	1,500	7,408
Palau	21,000	140,182
Papua New Guinea	7,744,700	152,705
Samoa	187,300	130,653
Solomon Islands	642,000	20,053
Tonga	103,300	20,199
Tuvalu	11,300	1,031
Vanuatu	262,000	108,656
Total		1,726,151

Source:
South Pacific Tourism Organization

with much more than tourism. For years the nation has had the strongest economy, and one of the most diversified, in the Pacific. Fiji's economy seems to be hinged on three sectors: exports of sugar, minerals, and other goods; substantial remittances over the last 20 years; and its expanding tourist industry. To Fiji in the list of standouts we might add Guam, with its 1,400,000 visitors, and the Northern Marianas with a 2015 total of 440,000 (Table 3).

The second tier—those groups with more than 100,000 visitors yearly—includes Palau, Cook Islands, Papua New Guinea, Samoa, and Vanuatu, in addition to French Polynesia and New Caledonia. But visitor numbers don't tell the whole story here. Palau and the Cooks both have a population of only about 20,000. Given their population bases and the size of their economies, the tourism industries they have built operate as strong economic forces in these two island groups (Figure 1). Both island groups, then, remain strong candidates for a bright future in tourism.

Samoa and Vanuatu each have a population about 10 times greater than Palau and the Cooks, and so tourism is a less potent but still significant economic force there (Hezel 2012, 16–17). In Papua New Guinea with its population of over 7 million, on the other hand, tourism barely registers as a factor in its economy. Vanuatu and Samoa have shown substantial growth and might be on the verge of creating a vibrant tourist industry someday (Figure 1).

Those at the bottom are the Marshalls, Kiribati, the FSM, Tuvalu, Tonga, and the Solomons. With visitor figures of fewer than 30,000 visitors yearly, they would seem doomed to building

Table 3. Tourism Arrivals ('000s), Pacific Islands: 1995–2015

	1995	2000	2005	2010	2015
American Samoa	34	44	24	23	14
CNMI	669	517	498	375	479
Cook Islands	48	73	85	102	124
Fiji	318	294	545	632	755
French Polynesia	172	252	208	154	181*
FSM	18	21	19	20	20
Guam	1,362	1,287	1,228	1,196	1,409
Kiribati	4	5	4	5	2*
Palau	53	58	86	92	168
Papua New Guinea	42	58	69	140	153*
Republic of the Marshall Islands	6	5	9	5	6
Samoa	68	88	102	122	137
Solomon Islands	12	5	9	21	20*
Tonga	29	35	42	47	20
Tuvalu	1	1	1	2	1
Vanuatu	44	58	62	97	90

Note:
2015 figures derived from national visitors' bureau websites. Figures with asterisks are for 2014.

Source:
World Bank (http://data.worldbank.org/indicator/ST.INT.ARVL).

Figure 1. Tourism receipts as percentage of GDP

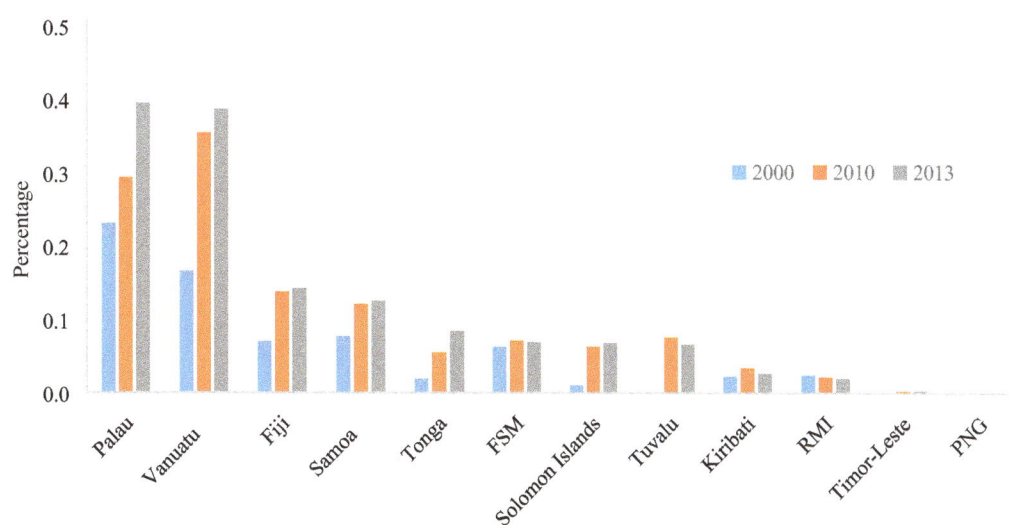

Source: World Development Indicators. http://data.worldbank.org/indicator.

The countries represented in Table 4 of the Conclusion are members of Pacific ACP and SPTO. In other words, they are the same countries and territories as those listed in Table 2 of this chapter.

economies without much help from tourism. In theory, of course, the situation in any of these places could change. Stardust might somehow be sprinkled on the land and a late-blooming tourist industry could spring up. But Table 3, showing rough visitor rates over the past 20 years, reveals that these island nations have shown little change over that period. Consequently, it would be difficult to imagine any of these nations becoming a major tourist destination in the future.

LIKELIHOOD OF EXPANSION

To determine the likelihood of the expansion of tourism throughout the Pacific, we should first consider the present composition of the market. The Pacific as a whole depends heavily on visitors from its nearby English-speaking neighbors to sustain its industry. Australian and New Zealand visitors comprise 53 percent of the whole market. Visitors from America and Europe make up another 22 percent, while Asians constitute only 17 percent of all visitors (Table 4). Hence, tourism in the Pacific is disproportionately reliant on Australia and New Zealand, two nations with a total population of less than 30 million, while remaining relatively unaffected by the expanding market in Asia.

Micronesia, located in the northwest Pacific and much closer to the main Asian centers, is a very different story. Visitor figures for Guam and CNMI together, as we have noted above, surpass those for the rest of the entire Pacific. The degree to which Micronesian destinations depend on the Asian market is clear from the breakdown of visitors by point of origin. The data provided on Palau and CNMI illustrate this vividly. Of Palau's 168,000 visitors in 2015, 144,000 were from Asia; thus, 86% of its visitor total came from this broad market. For CNMI the number is even higher: Asian visitors represented 93% of the total in 2015 (see the tables in the Palau and CNMI chapters, or Table 4 below).

Table 4. Tourist Markets for the Pacific Nations, 2014

	Visitors (2014)	% of Total
Australia	576,802	34
New Zealand	309,225	18
Pacific Islands	122,624	7
USA	167,887	10
Canada	27,277	1
Europe	190,905	11
Japan	84,534	5
China	62,728	4
Other Asia	135,235	8
Other countries	26,041	1
Total	1,703,258	

Note:
Table 2 nations are figured in the total in this table.

Source:
South Pacific Tourism Organization.

Asia is the market of the present and future for Micronesia. Yet, unless trends swing during coming years, tourism in the rest of the Pacific will continue to depend on the nearby markets of Australia and New Zealand, while a much smaller market from the United States and Europe will be divided among the countries of the South Pacific. If expansion of tourism in the Pacific is to occur, this shift to the Asian market will have to happen.

But will this change occur? Will the rest of the Pacific begin to benefit from Asian tourism, the consequence of the rapid economic growth of several Asian nations, as CNMI and Palau already have? Tourist fads change and trends are altered, so anything is possible. What does not change, however, is location. Eastern Asia is the great new market, almost boundless in size. Micronesia has benefitted from this market for years and is poised to do so in the foreseeable future. We have already noted how the strong link with Japan initially helped fashion CNMI and Palau into popular destinations for Asian tourists. Here we might look at the impact that geographic location of various Pacific Islands can have on air-travel cost since the latter is an important factor in choice of a vacation spot. Table 1 shows the comparative cost of discount tickets from key Asian cities to major Pacific Island destinations.

CNMI, Guam, and Palau are the only destinations that offer round-trip fares from Tokyo at less than $1,000, as Table 4 shows. The fares to these Micronesian vacation spots from Seoul and Beijing are higher, but still much cheaper than to other destinations in the Pacific. Costlier travel to other islands in the Pacific does not rule out the possibility of an expansion of Asian tourism into the more remote Pacific, but it should be viewed as a constraint upon such growth. In time, there could be a spillover of Asian tourism from Micronesia to the rest of the Pacific. To promote such expansion, we would do well to keep in mind some of the factors, discussed above, that were key in the growth of Asian-based tourism in Palau and CNMI.

In time, there could be a spillover of Asian tourism from Micronesia to the rest of the Pacific

IMPACT ON THE ISLAND ECONOMY

Tourism can become a critical component in the economy of a small-island nation, as it has in the case of Palau and the Cook Islands. If the thriving tourist industry is less critical to Fiji, that is only because its economy is more diversified than in most Pacific islands. In Figure 1 we can view the size of each Pacific Island national economy, as measured in GDP, against the gross income from that country's tourist industry. Not all of this gross income makes its way into the local economy, of course. This figure is a rough measure of the strength of the tourist industry, but it should not be taken as a real contribution to the national economy. For Palau in 2014, for instance, total tourism earnings were recorded as $135 million, but of this only an estimated $54 million entered the economy of Palau (Palau chapter, Table 3).

According to Figure 1, tourism shows the strongest impact in Palau and the Cook Islands, where tourism revenues measure 50 percent or more of the total GDP. Aside from Fiji, which has been discussed, there are only two other islands in which tourism revenues are significant: Vanuatu and Samoa. In all other cases tourism currently has a negligible impact on development of the national economy.

Tourism is an option for those blessed with the advantages needed to make it work. Pacific nations in search of a pathway to economic development should be encouraged to explore this option. Yet, a sense of realism is important here. Not every Pacific nation will be able to exploit tourism in the future. For those that do manage to generate a tourist industry, it can certainly make a substantial contribution, although it is probably too much to expect that tourism alone can propel a nation into full self-reliance.

REFERENCES

Hezel, Francis X. 1995. *Strangers in Their Own Land: A Century of Colonial Rule in the Caroline and Marshall Islands*. Pacific Islands Monograph Series, no. 13. Honolulu: University of Hawai'i Press.

———. 2012. *Pacific Island Nations: How Viable Are Their Economies?* Pacific Islands Policy, no. 7. Honolulu: East-West Center. https://www.eastwestcenter.org/publications/pacific-island-nations-how-viable-are-their-economies.

Oceania TV Network. 2015. "Charter Flights Reduced to Balance Tourism Market in Palau." March 6. http://www.oceaniatv.net/2015/03/06/charter-flights-reduced-to-balance-tourism-market-in-palau.

Osman, Wali M. 2000. *Republic of Palau: Economic Report*. Honolulu: Bank of Hawai'i and East-West Center.

US Department of State. 2013. "Investment Climate Statement – Palau." http://www.state.gov//e/eb/rls/othr/ics/2013/204586.htm.

US DOS. *See* US Department of State.

NOTES

[1] We can contrast the relative ease of getting Filipino labor into Palau with the problem of doing so in the nearby FSM. Because all flights to the FSM go through Guam, workers require a US visa and the further outlay of cash needed to fly to the national consular office to apply for renewal of the visa.

[2] Within the past 10 years, for instance, a Korean hotel was opened in Sapuk, one of the outlying villages on Weno, without difficulty. The hotel closed soon afterward for lack of business, but the partnership between the Korean and Chuukese partners continued as they explored new business opportunities.

[3] The economic report on Palau issued by the Bank of Hawai'i in 2000 offers a helpful overview of the land issues in Palau. It states that there were 8,540 unresolved land cases booked in the national land court. The court system has made some progress since, but at a relatively slow rate (Osman 2000, 18–19).

[4] New Caledonia and French Polynesia, along with American Samoa, are included since these territories are all members of the South Pacific Tourism Organization (SPTO). Guam and the CNMI, on the other hand, are not members.

Acknowledgments

A project of this nature is almost always the result of support from numerous sources. The Asian Development Bank's Pacific Division was responsible for funding this effort as part of a larger project examining economic linkages between the Pacific islands region and Asia. The East-West Center's Pacific Islands Development Program (PIDP) worked closely with the Asia Development Bank in conceptualizing and implementing this research endeavor. I am grateful to both organizations.

Some of the most valuable insights and information found in this report came from individuals who were exceptionally generous with their time. Although the names of interviewees are too numerous to mention here, they are found at the conclusion of each case study. I remain most grateful for the gracious hospitality that was extended to me. Any errors or omissions are the responsibility of the author.

About the Author

Francis X. Hezel is a Jesuit priest who has worked in Micronesia for nearly fifty years. He spent part of this time as a teacher, principal and director at Xavier High School, Chuuk. He also served as regional superior of the Jesuits in Micronesia. For 39 years he served as the director of Micronesian Seminar, a Jesuit-sponsored research-pastoral institute engaged in extensive community education work in the Pacific. In this capacity he has organized several conferences on current issues and has written and spoken widely about social change and its impact on island societies. He has also published nearly a hundred articles and eleven books on Micronesian history and culture, including *The First Taint of Civilization* and *Strangers in Their Own Land*. He produced over 70 video documentaries for local broadcast, including a seven-hour series on the history of Micronesia, and introduced a popular website that offers Micronesians everywhere the opportunity to access MicSem products and to discuss contemporary issues with one another.

www.ingramcontent.com/pod-product-compliance
Lightning Source LLC
Chambersburg PA
CBHW041319290326
41931CB00045B/3499